Born in Northern Ireland in 1931
best and most ingenious of Bri
worked as an engineer, in aircr
PR and journalism, Shaw has
since 1975, turning out highly professional, consistently
entertaining work.

By the same author

BOB SHAW

The Peace Machine

GRAFTON BOOKS

A Division of the Collins Publishing Group

LONDON GLASGOW
TORONTO SYDNEY AUCKLAND

Grafton Books
A Division of the Collins Publishing Group
8 Grafton Street, London W1X 3LA

Published by Grafton Books 1987

First published in Great Britain by Transworld Publishers Ltd
1976 as *Ground Zero Man*. This revised edition first published
by Victor Gollancz Ltd 1985

Copyright © Bob Shaw 1971, 1985

ISBN 0-586-06991-7

Printed and bound in Great Britain by
Collins, Glasgow

Set in Times

Prologue

My finger rests lightly on the black button.

The street beyond this window looks quiet, but I am not deceived – for my death lies out there, waiting. I had thought myself prepared to face it, yet now a strange timidity grips me. Having surrendered all claim to life, I am still reluctant to die. The only parallel to this mood in my experience is that of a man whose marriage is failing (of such things I can speak with some authority) but who lacks the nerve or energy for adultery. He eyes another woman squarely, with all the boldness he can muster, and inwardly he begs her to take the first step – for, in spite of his yearnings, he cannot. In this way then, I confront the sergeant whose arrest is so strict; in this way I hesitate on the threshold of one of death's ten thousand doors.

My finger rests lightly on the black button.

The sky, too, looks peaceful, but I wonder. Up there in that vault of wind-scoured pewter an aircraft may be preparing to unburden itself of a man-made sun; at this exact second a missile may be penetrating the upper atmosphere amid a cloud of decoys and slow-tumbling rocket casings. That way, the whole town would go with me, but my conscience can sustain the weight of seventy thousand deaths – as long as there is time to carry out the vow before the fireball comes billowing and spreading.

As long as I press the black button.

My left arm hangs limp, and blood trickles warmly downward across the palm of that hand, tempting me to close the fingers, to try holding on to life. I can find no bullet hole in the material of my sleeve – the fibres appear to have closed over it as do a bird's feathers – which seems strange, but what do I know of such things?

How did I, Lucas Hutchman, an undistinguished mathematician, come to be in this situation?

It should be instructive to consider the events of the past few weeks, but I'm tired and must be careful not to relax too much.

I must be prepared to press the black button . . .

1

Hutchman lifted the squared sheet from his desk, looked at it, and felt something very strange happen to his face.

Starting at the hairline, an icy sensation moved downward in a slow wave over his forehead, cheeks, and chin. The skin in the region of the wave prickled painfully as he felt each pore open and close in an insubstantial progression, like wind patterns on a field of grain. He put a hand to his forehead and found it slippery, dewed with chill perspiration.

A cold sweat, he thought, his shocked mind seizing gratefully on the irrelevant. *You really can break into a cold sweat – and I thought it was just a figure of speech.*

He mopped his face and then stood up, feeling strangely weak. The squared sheet on the desk reflected sunlight up at him, seeming to glow malevolently. He stared at the close-packed strings of figures he had put there, and his consciousness ricocheted away from what they represented. *What unimpressive handwriting! In some places the figures are three, four times bigger than in others. Surely that must show lack of character.*

Vague colours – mauve and saffron – drifted beyond the frosted-glass partition which separated him from his secretary. He snatched the rectangle of paper and crammed it into his jacket pocket, but the area of colour was moving towards the corridor, not coming his way. Hutchman opened the connecting door and peered through at Muriel Burnley. She had the cautious, prissy face of a village postmistress, and an incongruously voluptuous figure which was nothing but a source of embarrassment to her.

'Are you going out?' Hutchman said the first words that came into his head, meanwhile looking unhappily around her office which was too small, and choked with olive-green filing cabinets. The travel posters and plants with which Muriel had decorated it served only to increase the atmosphere of claustrophobia. She glanced with resentful perplexity at her right hand on the knob of the outer door, at the coffee cup and foil-wrapped chocolate bar in her left hand, and at the clock which registered 10:30 – the time at which she always took her break with another secretary along the corridor. She did not speak.

'I just wanted to know if Don's in this morning,' Hutchman extemporized. Don Spain was a cost account-ant who had the office on the opposite side of Muriel's and shared her services.

'Him!' Muriel's face was scornful behind the tinted prescription lenses – the exact colour of antique-brown glass – which screened her eyes from the world. 'He won't be in for another half-hour – this is Thursday.'

'What happens on Thursday?'

'This is the day he works at his other job.' Muriel spoke with heavy patience.

'Oh!' Hutchman recalled that Spain made up the pay-roll for a small bakery on the far side of town as a sideline and usually handed his work in on Thursdays. Having outside employment was, as Muriel frequently pointed out, a breach of company regulations, but the main cause of her anger was that Spain often gave her letters to type on behalf of the bakery. 'All right, then. You run along and have your coffee.'

'I was going to,' Muriel assured him, closing the door firmly behind her.

Hutchman went back into his own office and took the sheet of figures from his pocket. He held it by one corner above the metal waste bin and ignited it with his bulky desk cigarette lighter. The paper had begun to burn reluctantly, with a surprising amount of acrid smoke, when the door to Muriel's office was opened. Shades of grey moved on the frosted glass, the blurred mask of a face looking his way. Hutchman dropped the paper, stamped it out, and crammed it back into his pocket in one frantic movement. A second later Spain looked into the office, grinning his conspiratorial grin.

'Ho there, Hutch,' he said huskily. 'How're you getting on?'

'Not bad.' Hutchman was flustered and aware he was showing it. 'Not badly, I mean.'

Spain's grin widened as he sensed he was on to something. He was a short, balding, untidy man with slate-grey jowls and an almost pathological desire to know everything possible about the private lives of his colleagues. His preference was for material of a scandalous nature, but failing that any kind of information was almost equally acceptable. Over the years Hutchman had developed a fascinated dread of the little man and his patient, ferreting methods.

'Anybody asking about me this morning?' Spain came right into the office.

'Not that I know of. You're safe for another week.'

Spain recognized the gibe about his outside work and his eyes locked knowingly with Hutchman's for an instant. Suddenly Hutchman felt contaminated, wished he had not made the reference which somehow had associated him with Spain's activities.

'What's the smell in here?' Spain's face appeared concerned. 'Something on fire?'

'The waste bin was smouldering. I threw a butt into it.'

Spain's eyes shone with gleeful disbelief. 'Did you, Hutch? Did you? You might have burned the whole factory down.'

Hutchman shrugged, picked up a file from his desk, and began studying its contents. It was a summary of performance data from a test firing of a pair of Jack-and-Jill missiles. He had already abstracted as much information as he required from it, but he hoped Spain would take the hint and leave.

'Were you watching television last night?' Spain said, his throaty voice slurring with pleasure.

'Can't remember.' Hutchman shuffled graph papers determinedly.

'Did you see that blonde bit on the Mort Walters show? The one that's supposed to be a singer?'

'No.' Hutchman was fairly sure he had seen the girl in question, but he had no desire to get involved in a conversation – in any case, his viewing time had been brief. He had glanced up from a book and noticed an unusually pneumatic female figure on the screen, then Vicky had walked into the room and switched the set off. Accusation and disgust had spread like Arctic ice across her features. He had waited all evening for an explosion, but this time she seemed to be burning on a slow fuse.

'Singer!' Spain said indignantly. 'It isn't hard to see how she got on that show. I thought those balloons of hers were going to come right out every time she took a breath.'

What's going on here? Hutchman thought. *That's exactly what Vicky said last night. What are they getting steamed up about? And why do they get at me about it? I've never exercised the* droit du *casting director.*

'. . . makes me laugh is all the fuss about too much violence on television,' Spain was saying. 'They never stop to think about what seeing all these half-naked women does to a kid's mind.'

'Probably makes them think about sex,' Hutchman said stonily.

'Of course it does!' Spain was triumphant. 'What did I tell you?'

Hutchman closed his eyes. *This . . . this thing standing before me is an adult member of the so-called human race. God help us. Now is the time for all good parties to come to the aid of the men. Vicky gets jealous of electron patterns on a cathode-ray tube. Spain prefers to see shadows of the Cambodian war – those tortured women holding dead babies with the blue-rimmed bullet holes in their downy skulls. But would this charred sheet of paper in my pocket really change anything? I CAN MAKE NEUTRONS DANCE TO A NEW TUNE – but what about the chorea which affects humanity?*

'. . . all at it, all those whores you see on the box are at it. All on the game. I wish I'd been born a woman, that's all I can say. I'd have made a fortune.' Spain gave a throaty laugh.

Hutchman opened his eyes. 'Not from me, you wouldn't.'

'Am I not your type, Hutch? Not intellectual enough?'

Hutchman glanced at the large varnished pebble he used for a paperweight and imagined smashing Spain's head with it *Plea: justifiable insecticide.* 'Get out of my office, Don – I have work to do.'

Spain sniffed, producing a glutinous click in the back of his nose, and went through into the connecting office, closing the door behind him. The grey abstract of his figure on the frosted glass hovered in the region of Muriel's desk for a few minutes, accompanied by the sound of drawers being opened and papers riffled, then faded as he moved into his own room. Hutchman watched the pantomime with increasing self-disgust for the way in which he had never once come right out and told Spain what he thought of him. *I can make neutrons dance to a new tune, but I shrink from telling a human tick to fasten*

11

onto someone else. He took a bulky file marked 'secret' from the secure drawer of his desk and tried to concentrate on the project which was paying his salary.

Jack was a fairly conventional ground-to-air missile employing the simplest possible guidance-and-control system, that of radio command from the firing station. It was, in fact, a modification of an earlier Westfield defensive missile which had suffered from an ailment common to its breed – loss of control sensitivity as the distance between it and the launcher/control console complex increased. Westfield had conceived the idea of transferring part of the guidance-and-control system to a second missile – Jill – fired a fraction of a second later, which would follow Jack and relay data on its position relative to a moving target. The system was an attempt to preserve the simplicity of command-link guidance and yet obtain the accuracy of a fully automated target-seeking device. If it worked it would have a respectable range, high reliability, and low unit cost. As a senior mathematician with Westfield, Hutchman was engaged on rationalizing the maths, paring down the variables to a point where Jack and Jill could be directed by something not very different from a conventional fire-control computer.

The work was of minimal interest to him – being a far cry from the formalism of quantum mechanics – but the Westfield plant was close to Vicky's hometown. She refused to consider moving to London, or Cambridge (there had been a good offer from Brock at the Cavendish), or any other centre where he could have followed his own star; and he was too committed to their marriage to think about separating. Consequently he worked on the mathematics of many-particle systems in his spare time, more for relaxation than anything else. Relaxation! The thoughts he had been trying to suppress twisted upward from a lower level of his mind.

Our own government, the Russians, the Americans, the Chinese, the French – any and all of them would snuff me out in a second if they knew what is in my pocket. I can make neutrons dance to a new tune!

Shivering slightly, he picked up a pencil and began work, but concentration was difficult. After a futile hour he phoned the chief photographer and arranged a showing of all recent film on the Jack-and-Jill test firings.

In the cool anonymous darkness of the small theatre scenes of water and grainy blue sky filled his eyes, became the only reality, making him feel disembodied. The dark smears of the missiles hovered and trembled and swooped, exhausting clouds of hydraulic fluid into the air at every turn, until their motors flared out and they dropped into the sea, slowly, swinging below the orange mushrooms of their recovery chutes. *Jack fell down and broke his crown, and Jill . . .*

'They'll never be operational,' a voice said in his ear. It was that of Boyd Crangle, assistant chief of preliminary design, who had come into the room unnoticed by Hutchman. Crangle had been opposed to the Jack-and-Jill project from its inception.

'Think not?'

'Not a chance,' Crangle said with crisp confidence. 'All the aluminium we use in this country's aerospace industry – it ends up being melted down and made into garbage cans because our aircraft and missiles are obsolescent before they get into the air. That's what you and I help to produce, Hutch. Garbage cans. It would be much better, more honest, and probably more profitable if we cut out the intermediate stage and went into full-scale manufacture of garbage cans.'

'Or ploughshares.'

'Or what?'

'The things we ought to beat our swords into.'

13

'Very profound, Hutch.' Crangle sighed heavily. 'It's almost lunchtime – let's go out to the Duke and have a pint.'

'No thanks, Boyd. I'm going home for lunch, taking half a day off.' Hutchman was mildly surprised by his own words, but realized he really did need to get away for a few hours on his own and face the fact that the equations he had written on a single scrap of paper could make him the most important man in the world. There were decisions to be made.

The drive to Crymchurch took less than half an hour on clear, almost-empty roads which looked slightly unfamiliar through being seen at an unfamiliar time of day. It was a fresh October afternoon and the air which lapped at the open windows of the car was cool. Turning into the avenue where he lived, Hutchman was suddenly struck by the fact that autumn had arrived – the sidewalks were covered with leaves, gold and copper coins strewn by extravagant beeches. *September gets away every year,* he thought. *The favourite month always runs through my fingers before I realize it's begun.*

He parked outside the long, low house which had been a wedding present from Vicky's father. Her car was missing from the garage which probably meant she was shopping in the town before picking up David at school. He had deliberately avoided calling her to say he would be home. When Vicky was working up to an emotional explosion it was very difficult for Hutchman to think constructively about anything, and this afternoon he wanted his mind to be cold and dark as an ancient wine cellar. Even as he let himself into the house the thought of his wife triggered a spray of memory shards, fragments of the past stained with the discordant hues of old angers and half-forgotten disappointments. (The time she had found Muriel's home-telephone number in his pocket and convinced herself he was having an affair: *I'll kill you, Luke* – steak knife's serrated edge suddenly pressed into his neck, her eyes inhuman as pebbles – *I know what's going on between you and that fat tart, and I'm not going to let you get away with it* . . . another occasion: a computer operator had haemorrhaged in the office and he had driven her home – *Why did she come to you? You helped her to get rid of something!* . . . a receding series of mirrored bitternesses: *How dare you suggest there's anything wrong with my mind! Is a woman insane if she doesn't want a filthy disease brought into the house, to her and her child?* David's eyes beseeching him, lenses of tears: *Are you and Mum going to separate, Dad? Don't leave.* I'll do without pocket money. I'll never wet my pants again.)

Hutchman put the past aside with an effort. In the coolness of the kitchen he hesitated for a moment then decided he could do without eating. He went into the bedroom, changed his business clothes for slacks and a close-fitting shirt, and took his archery equipment from a closet. The lustrous laminated woods of the bow were glass-smooth to his touch. He carried the gear out to the back of the house, wrestled the heavy target of coiled-straw rope out of the toolshed and set it on its tripod. The original garden had not been long enough to accommodate a hundred-yard green, so he had bought an extra piece of ground and removed part of the old hedge. With the target in place, he began the soothing near-Zen ritual of the shooting – placing the silver studs in the turf to mark the positions of his feet, stringing and adjusting the bow, checking the six arrows for straightness, arranging them in the ground quiver. The first arrow he fired ascended cleanly, flashed sunlight once at the top of its trajectory, and dwindled from sight. A moment later he heard it strike with a firm note which told him it was close to centre. His binoculars confirmed that the shaft was in the blue at about seven o'clock.

Pleased at having judged the effect of the humidity on the bow's cast so closely, he fired two more sighting-in arrows, making fine adjustments on the windage and elevation screws of the bowsight. He retrieved the arrows and settled in to shoot a York Round, meticulously filling in the points scored in his record book. As the round progressed one part of his mind became utterly absorbed in the struggle for perfection, and another turned to the question of how well qualified Lucas Hutchman was to play the role of God.

On the technical level the situation was diamond-sharp, uncomplicated. He was in a position to translate the figures scribbled on his charred sheet into physical reality. Doing so would necessitate several weeks' work on thousands of pounds' worth of electrical and electronic components, and the result would be a small, rather unimpressive machine.

But it would be a machine which, if switched on, would almost instantaneously detonate every nuclear device on Earth.

It would be an antibomb machine.

An antiwar machine.

An instrument for converting megadeaths into megalives.

The realization that a neutron resonator could be built had come to Hutchman one calm Sunday morning almost a year earlier. He had been testing some ideas concerned with the solution of the many-particle time-independent Schrödinger equation when – quite suddenly, by a trick of conceptual parallax – he saw deeper than ever before into the mathematical forest which screens reality from reason. A tree lane seemed to open in the thickets of

Hermite polynomials, eigenvectors, and Legendre functions; and shimmering at its farthest end, for a brief second, was the antibomb machine. The path closed again almost at once, but Hutchman's flying pencil was recording enough of the landmarks, the philosophical map references, to enable him to find his way back again at a later date.

Accompanying the flash of inspiration was a semimystical feeling that he had been chosen, that he was the vehicle for another's ideas. He had read about the phenomenon of the sense of *givenness* which often accompanies breakthroughs in human thought, but the feeling was soon obscured by considerations of the social and professional implications. Like the minor poet who produced a single, never-to-be-repeated classic, like a forgotten artist who has created one deathless canvas – Lucas Hutchman, an unimportant mathematician, could make an indelible mark on history. If he dared.

The year had not been one of steady progress. There was one period when it seemed that the energy levels involved in producing self-propagating neutron resonance would demand several times the planet's electrical power output, but the obstacle had proved illusory. The machine would, in fact, be adequately supplied by a portable powerpack, its signals relaying themselves endlessly from neutron to neutron, harmlessly and imperceptibly except where they encountered concentrations close to critical mass. Then there had come a point where he dreamed that the necessary energy levels were so *low* that a circuit diagram might become the actual machine, powered by minute electrical currents induced in the pencil lines by stray magnetic fields. *Or could it be,* he wondered in the vision, *that merely visualizing the completed circuitry would build an effective analogue of the machine in my brain cells? Then would mind find its true ascendancy over matter – one dispassionate intellectual thrust and every nuclear stockpile in the world would consume its masters . . .*

But that danger faded too; the maths was complete, and now Hutchman was face-to-face with the realization that he wanted nothing to do with his own creation.

Voice from another dimension, intruding: You're fired six dozen arrows at a hundred yards for a total of 402 points. *The neutron resonator is the ultimate defense.* That's your highest score ever for the range. *And in the context of nuclear warfare the ultimate defence can be regarded as the ultimate weapon.* Keep this up and you'll top the thousand for the round. *If I breathe a word of this to the Ministry of Defence I'll sink without a trace, into one of those discreet establishments in the heart of 'The Avengers' country.* You've been chasing that thousand a long time, Hutch – four years or more. *And what about Vicky? She'd go mad. And David?* Pull up the studs, and ground quiver, and move down to eighty yards – and keep cool. *The balance of nuclear power does exist, after all – who could shoulder the responsibility of disrupting it? It's been forty-three years since World War Two, and it's becoming obvious that nobody's actually going to use the bomb. In any case, didn't the Japanese who were incinerated by napalm outnumber those unfortunates at H and N?* Raise the sight to the eighty-yard mark, nock the arrow, relax and breathe, draw easily, keep your left elbow out, kiss the string, watch your draw length, bowlimb vertical, ring sight centred on the gold, hold it, hold it, hold it . . .

'Why aren't you at the office, Luke?' Vicky's voice sounded only inches behind him.

Hutchman watched his arrow go wide, hit the target close to the rim, and almost pass clear through the less tightly packed straw.

'I didn't hear you arrive,' he said evenly. He turned and examined her face, aware she had startled him deliberately but wanting to find out if she was issuing a forthright challenge or was simulating innocence. Her rust-coloured eyes met his at once, like electrical contacts finding sockets, an interface of hostility.

All right, he thought. 'Why did you sneak up on me like that? You ruined a shot.'

She shrugged, wide clavicles seen with da Vincian clarity in the tawny skin of her shoulders. 'You can play archery all evening.'

'One doesn't *play* archery – how many times have I . . . ?'

He steadied his temper. Misuse of the word was one of her oldest tricks. 'What do you want, Vicky?'

'I want to know why you're not at the office this afternoon.' She examined the skin of her upper arms critically as she spoke, frowning at the summer's fading tan which even yet was deeper than the amber of her sleeveless dress, face darkened with shadows of the introspective and secret alarms that beautiful women sometimes appear to feel when looking at their own bodies. 'I suppose I'm entitled to hear.'

'I couldn't take it this afternoon.' *I can make neutrons dance to a new tune.* 'All right?'

'How nice for you.' Disapproval registered briefly on the smooth-planed face, like smoke passing across the sun. 'I wish I could stop work when I feel like it.'

'You're in a better position – you only start when you feel like it.'

'Funny man! Have you had lunch?'

'I'm not hungry. I'll stay here and finish this round.' Hutchman wished desperately that Vicky would leave. In spite of the wasted shot he could still break the four-figure barrier provided he could shut out the universe, treat every arrow as though it were the last. The air was immobile, the sun burned steadily on the ringed target, and suddenly he understood that the eighty yards of lawn were an unimportant consideration. There came a vast certitude that he could feather the next arrow in the exact geometrical centre of the gold and clip its fletching with the others – if he could be left in peace.

'I see. You want to go into one of your trances. Who will you imagine you're with – Trisha Garland?'

'Trisha Garland?' A bright-red serpent of irritation stirred in the pool of his mind, clouding the waters. 'Who the hell's Trisha Garland?'

'As if you didn't know!'

'I've no idea who the lady is.'

'Lady! That's good, calling that one a lady – the bedwarmer who can't sing a note and wouldn't know a lady if she saw one.'

Hutchman almost gaped – his wife must be referring to the singer he had glimpsed on television the previous evening – then a bitter fury engulfed him. *You're sick*, he raged inwardly. *You're so sick that just being near you is making me sick*. Aloud he said, calmly: 'The last thing I want out here is somebody singing while I shoot.'

'Oh, you *do* know who I mean.' Vicky's face was triumphant beneath its massive helm of copper hair. 'Why did you pretend you didn't know her?'

'Vicky.' Hutchman turned his back on her. 'Please put the lid back on the cesspit you have for a mind – then go away from me before I drive one of these arrows through your head.'

He nocked another arrow, drew, and aimed at the target. Its shimmering concentricities seemed very distant across an ocean of malicious air currents. He fired and knew he had plucked the string instead of achieving a clean release, even before the bow gave a discordant, disappointed twang, even before he saw the arrow fly too high and pass over the target. The single ugly word he spat out failed to relieve the tensions racking his body, and he began unbuckling his leather armguard, pulling savagely at the straps.

'I'm sorry, darling.' Vicky sounded contrite, like a child, as her arms came snaking round him from behind. 'I can't help it if I'm jealous of you.'

'Jealous!' Hutchman gave a shaky laugh, making the shocked discovery that he was close to tears. 'If you found me kissing another woman and didn't like it, that would be jealousy. But when you build up fantasies about people you see on the box, torture yourself, and take it out on me – that's something else.'

'I love you so much I don't want you even to *see* another woman.' Vicky's right hand slipped downward, purposefully, from his waist to his groin, and at the same instant he became aware of the pressure of her breasts in the small of his back. She rested her head between his shoulder blades. 'David isn't home from school yet.'

I'm a fool if I fall for this so easily, he told himself; but at the same time he kept thinking about the rare event of the house being empty and available for unrestrained love-making, which was what she had been suggesting. She loved him so much she didn't want him even to look at another woman – put that way, under these circumstances, it sounded almost reasonable. With Vicky's tight belly thrust determinedly against his buttocks, he could almost convince himself it was his own fault for inspiring such devouring passion in her. He turned and allowed himself to be kissed, planning to cheat, to give his body and withhold his mind, but as they walked back to the house he realized he had been beaten once again. After eight years of marriage, her attraction for him had increased to the point where he could not even imagine having a sexual relationship with another woman.

'It's a hell of a handicap to be naturally monogamous,' he grumbled, setting his equipment down outside the rear door. 'I get taken advantage of.'

'Poor thing.' Vicky walked into the kitchen ahead of him and began to undress as soon as he had closed the door. He followed her to their bedroom, shedding his own clothes as he went. As they lay together he slid his hands under her and clamped one on each shoulder, then secured her feet by pressing upwards on the soles with his insteps, immobilizing his wife in the physical analogue of the mental curbs he had never been able to place on her. And when it was all over he lay dreamily beside her, completely without *triste*, hovering deliciously between sleep and wakefulness. The world outside was the world he had known as a boy lying in bed late on a summer's morning, listening to the quiet sanity of barely heard garden conversations, milk bottles clashing in the street, the measured stroke of a hand-operated lawnmower in the distance. He felt secure. The bomb, the whole nuclear doom concept, was outdated, a little old-fashioned, along with John Foster Dulles and Senator McCarthy, ten-inch television sets and razor-edge Triumph cars, the New Look, and the white gulls of flying boats over The Solent. We passed a vital milestone back in July '66 – the month in which the interval between World War One and World War Two separated us from V-J Day. *Looking at it dispassionately, from the historical pinnacle of 1988, one can't even imagine them dropping the bomb . . .*

Hutchman was roused by a hammering on the front door, and guessed that his son had arrived home from school. He threw on some clothes, leaving Vicky dozing in bed, and hurried to the door. David crowded in past him wordlessly – brown hair tousled, scented with

22

October air – dropped his schoolbag with a leathery thud and clink of buckles, and vanished into the toilet without closing the door. His disappearance was followed by the sound of churning water and exaggerated sighs of relief. Still suffused with relaxed optimism, Hutchman grinned as he picked up the schoolbag and put it in a closet. *There are levels of reality,* he thought, *and this one is just as valid as any other. Perhaps Vicky is right – perhaps the greatest and most dangerous mistake an inhabitant of the global village can make is to start feeling responsible for his neighbours ten thousand miles away. No nervous system yet evolved can cope with the guilts of others.*

'Dad?' David's smile was ludicrous because of its ragged emerging teeth. 'Are we going to the stock-car racing tonight?'

'I don't know, son. It's a little late in the year – the evenings are cold out at the track.'

'Can't we wear overcoats, and eat hot dogs and things like that to keep warm?'

'You know something? You're right! Let's do that.' Hutchman watched the slow spread of pleasure across the boy's face. *Decision made and ratified,* he thought. *The neutrons can wait for another dancing master. Now stir the fire and close the shutters fast . . .* He went into the bedroom and roused Vicky. 'Get up, woman. David and I want an early dinner – we're going to the stock-car racing.'

Vicky straightened, pulled the white linen sheet tight around herself, and lay perfectly still, hipless as an Egyptian mummy. 'I'm not moving till you tell me you love me.'

Hutchman crossed to the bed. 'I do love you.'

'And you'll never look at anyone else?'

'I'll never look at anyone else.'

Vicky smiled languorously. 'Come back to bed.'

23

Hutchman shook his head. 'David's home.'

'Well, he has to learn the facts of life sometime.'

'I know, but I don't want him writing an essay about us for the school. I've been branded as a drunkard since the one he did last month, and I'll be expelled from the PTA if word gets around that I'm a sex maniac.'

'Oh, well.' Vicky sat up and rubbed her eyes. 'I think I'll go to the stock-car racing with you.'

'But you don't enjoy it.'

'I think I'll enjoy it tonight.'

Suspecting that Vicky was trying to atone for the scene in the garden, but gratified nonetheless, Hutchman left the room. He spent an hour in his study tidying up loose ends of correspondence. When he judged dinner was almost ready he went into the lounge and mixed a long and rather weak whisky and soda. David was at the television set, working with the channel-selector buttons. Hutchman sat down and took a sip from his glass, allowing himself to relax as the greens of the poplars outside darkened slightly in preparation for evening. The sky beyond the trees was filled with dimension after dimension of tumbled clouds, kingdoms of pink coral, receding towards infinity.

'Bloody hell,' David muttered, punching noisily at the channel selectors.

'Take it easy,' Hutchman said tolerantly. 'You're going to wreck the set altogether. What's the trouble?'

'I turned on "Grange Hill", and all I got was that.' David's face was scornful as he indicated the blank, gently flickering screen.

'Well you've got lines on the screen so they must be broadcasting a carrier wave – perhaps you're too early.'

'I'm not. It's always on at this time.'

Hutchman set his drink aside and went to the set. He was reaching for the fine-tuning control when the face of

24

a news reporter appeared abruptly on the screen. The man's eyes were grave as he read from a single sheet of paper.

'At approximately five o'clock this afternoon a nuclear device was exploded over the city of Damascus, capital of Syria. The force of the explosion was, according to preliminary estimates, approximately six megatons. The entire city is reported to be a mass of flame, and it is believed that the majority of Damascus's population of 550,000 have lost their lives in the holocaust.

'There is, as yet, no indication as to whether the explosion was the result of an accident or an act of aggression, but an emergency meeting of the Cabinet has been called at Westminster, and the Security Council of the United Nations will meet shortly in New York.

'This channel has suspended its regular programmes, but stay tuned for further bulletins, which will be broadcast as soon as reports are received.' The face faded quickly.

As he knelt before the blank, faintly hissing screen, Hutchman felt the newly familiar sensation of cold perspiration breaking out on his forehead.

2

Avoiding his son's perplexed gaze, Hutchman walked slowly into the kitchen. Vicky was standing with her back to him as she prepared the meal. She was singing and, as usual, looking slightly out of place in a role of such utter domesticity. He hated having to destroy the evening they had wrested from the day's misery.

'Vicky,' he said, almost guiltily. 'Something has happened. I just heard a news flash on the television. They say Damascus has been wiped out by a hydrogen bomb.'

'How awful.' Vicky turned, her hands full of diced cheese, and nodded towards a glass-fronted cupboard. 'How ghastly. Be a darling and reach me down the small casserole. Does it mean there's a war?'

He found the Pyrex dish mechanically and set it on the counter. 'They don't know who's responsible yet, but there could be half a million dead. Half a million!'

'It was bound to happen sooner or later. Shall I make a salad?'

'Salad? I . . . Do we still want to eat?'

'What do you expect us to do?' Vicky examined him curiously. 'Lucas, I do hope you're not going to go all egotistical over this.'

'Egotistical?'

'Yes – your famous seeing-every-sparrow-fall bit. There isn't one person in the world who would benefit from your having a nervous breakdown, but that doesn't stop you assuming responsibility for things happening ten thousand miles away.'

'Damascus is more like two thousand miles.'

'It wouldn't matter if it was two hundred miles.' Vicky slammed the casserole down, sending a flat, ghostly billow of flour along the counter. 'Lucas, you aren't even concerned with what happens next door, so kindly do us all a favour and . . .'

'I'm hungry,' David announced from the doorway. 'And what time are we going out?'

Hutchman shook his head. 'I'm sorry, son – we'll have to call it off for tonight.'

'Huh?' David's jaw sagged theatrically. 'But you said . . .'

'I know, but we can't go tonight.'

'Why not?' Vicky asked. 'I hope you don't think I'm going to sit in front of that television set all evening, listening to Robin Day and a band of experts who have no idea what's going to happen next telling us what's going to happen next. We promised David we were going to the stock-car racing so we're going.'

A mural of shattered, tortured bodies pulsed momentarily in Hutchman's vision. He followed David back into the lounge, where the television set still exhibited its slow-rolling flickers, and sat down. David punched the channel selector, got a vintage-comedy film and squatted contentedly to watch it. Amazed and slightly reassured at finding a normal programme on the air, Hutchman picked up his drink and allowed his consciousness to sink into the screen. A frantic motor chase was taking place along the sparse, sunny avenues of Hollywood in the Twenties. Hutchman ignored the central characters and studied the inhospitable frame buildings blistering in the lost sunshine. To his eyes they resembled sheds more than houses, yet they had been real, and by watching them closely he sometimes observed fragments of real lives recorded in the ancient celluloid. Anonymous lives, of dripping iceboxes and giant radios with fretted wooden

27

cases, but filled with the security of a past in which the worst that could happen to one was a few years on the breadline or, in wartime, a comprehensible death from machine-gun fire.

I've got to do it, Hutchman thought. *I've got to make the neutrons dance.*

Following the vintage movie was a string of commercials, more normality chopped up small. He was beginning to relax when the television screen went blank and abruptly came to life again. A mushroom cloud, roiling but motionless, sculptured, the white cubical buildings of Damascus hidden under its billowing fronds. The picture juddered and swung, obviously taken from a helicopter not equipped with camera mounts. Music filled the room, strident and urgent. *That damned apocalyptic jangling,* he thought. *Couldn't they have left it out for once? This isn't a dock strike or one of those eternal grey trade-union conferences.* A news reporter appeared and began to speak, quickly and soberly. He repeated the basic known facts, adding that the death roll was estimated at 400,000, and went on to sketch the feverish diplomatic activity in various capitals. Further down the story came an item which, in Hutchman's estimation, should have been one of the major headlines: 'It is now believed that the nuclear bomb was not delivered by a missile or by a military aircraft. Reports indicate that it was on board a civil airliner which was passing over the city, making its approach to Mezze airport seven kilometers to the southwest, when the detonation occurred.

'The seat of Syrian government has been transferred to Aleppo, where offers of immediate aid and messages expressing shock and sympathy have already been received from all Middle Eastern countries, including

Israel and the members of the League of Arab States, from which Syria withdrew in April last year.

'All branches of the Syrian armed forces have been fully mobilized, but in the absence of any obvious aggressor no military action has yet been undertaken. The entire country is in a state of stunned grief and resentment . . .'

Vicky passed between Hutchman and the screen. 'What's the latest? Is there going to be a war?'

'I don't know. It looks as though the bomb was on a civil airliner, so some guerrilla organization could be behind it – and there's a dozen or more for the Syrians to pick from.'

'So there isn't going to be a war.'

'Who knows? What do you call it when guerrillas can do a thing like that? They've graduated from rocket attacks on nursery schools to . . . to . . .'

'I mean a war that involves us.' Vicky's voice was sharp, reminding him he was not permitted to indulge in vicarious guilt.

'No, darling,' he said heavily. 'The human race may be involved – but not us.'

'Oh, God,' Vicky whispered. 'Pour me a drink, Lucas. This looks like being a long hard evening.'

As soon as they had finished eating, Hutchman went into the hall and looked up the number of the stadium where stock-car racing was held. He dialled it and listened to the blurry ringing tone long enough to convince himself there was going to be no reply. Just as he was putting the handset down it clicked.

'Hello,' a man's voice said hoarsely. 'Bennett here.'

'Hello, Crymchurch Stadium?' Hutchman had been so certain there would be no reply, he was temporarily lost for words.

'That's right.' The voice sounded suspicious. 'Is that you, Bert.'

'No.' Hutchman took a deep breath. 'I'm calling to see if the stock-car racing will still be taking place tonight.'

'Course it will, old son.' The man's chuckle was like nails being shaken in a bucket. 'Why shouldn't it be? The weather's just right, isn't it?'

'I guess so. I just wanted to make sure – the way things are . . .' Hutchman set the phone down and stood staring at his reflection in a gold-tinted mirror. *The weather's just right – no sign of fallout.*

'Who were you calling?' Vicky had opened the kitchen door and was looking out at him.

'The stadium,' he said.

'Why?'

Hutchman longed to ask her if it really made no difference to anybody, one major city more or less. 'Checking the time of the first race.'

She eyed him soberly then moved away into the kitchen, her own insular universe, and a moment later he heard her singing as she tidied up after the meal. David emerged from the kitchen, his jaws working furiously, and he went into his bedroom trailing a faint aroma of spearmint. Hutchman tried hard to play the game.

'David,' he shouted. 'What did I tell you about eating chewing gum?'

'You told me not to eat it.'

'Well then?'

For a reply David gave the gum some extra loud chomps which were plainly audible through the closed door. Hutchman shook his head in reluctant admiration. His son was as indomitable as only a healthy seven-year-old can be. *But how many indomitable seven-year-olds had died in Damascus? Six thousand or so? And how*

30

about the equally indomitable six-year-olds, and the five-year-olds, and the . . . ?

'Leave David alone,' Vicky said, passing him on her way into their bedroom. 'What harm will a little chewing gum do him?'

The walls, which had been falling towards Hutchman, shrank back into place. 'You know he always swallows the stuff.' He forced his lips to form the words, his mind to accommodate the domestic triviality. 'It's totally indigestible.'

'What of it? Come and help me dress.' He followed her into the bedroom, shamming response to the coquetry, setting his course on the oceans of time which would have to be crossed before he could lie down and lose himself in sleep.

The attendance at the stadium was about average for the time of year. Hutchman sat aloof in the airy darkness of the stand, unable to derive any warmth from the presence of his wife and son, unable to comprehend the spectacle of slithering, jouncing, colliding vehicles. When finally he got to bed sleep came almost immediately.

Dream universes spun like roulette wheels, unreality and reality flowed and sifted through each other, producing transient amalgams, solarized colours darting and spreading among crystal lattices of probability. Hutchman is a soldier – strangely, because he had never been in the army – and he is walking through the narrow, congested streets of an Eastern city. He has a companion, another soldier, and the city is . . . Damascus. Naturally Damascus. Hadn't something awful happened there? Something unthinkable? But the city is not quite real. All perspectives are choked, claustrophobic – this is the Middle East of a low-budget movie. The heat and dust are real enough, though. A kind of market square – and there's a woman. A Rita Moreno type of woman.

31

Hutchman and the other soldier speak to her, boldly, making their desires clear without actually stating them. The woman laughs delightedly, then invites them to come home and have stew with her family. *You're on, Hutch* – if only the other soldier would remove his insensitive, intruding presence. But he won't. There is rivalry there, much overplayed gallantry, displays of coarse wit mingled with, supposedly, unconcealable flashes of genuine warm attraction. Very much the mixture as before, but the woman enjoys it . . .

Her house is a dark place. Small rooms and walls that seem to be made of nothing else but carpets – oh, this is vintage Abbott-and-Costello stuff. Although the woman is real. Real enough, anyway. As she sits down on the floor her navel is lost among small, satisfying rolls of fat. Her mother is predictably huge and motherly, moving about, putting a black-iron pot of water on an open fire in the centre of the room. She adds vegetables to the water in the pot, smiles, begins stirring it, and it smells good. Hutchman and the other soldier are still jockeying for the woman, *but suddenly he notices there is a big, pale green lizard swimming around in the pot.* He has not seen the mother dropping it in, but he announces that he could not eat any of the stew. Immediately the woman is concerned. It's all right, she assures him – that isn't a real lizard.

It looks real to me.

No. We've been making this kind of stew around here for thousands of years, always with the same ingredients. And every time the mixture reaches the boil one of these things appears in it. They simply *happen*. Spontaneously.

I still say it's a real lizard.

It isn't – it has no soul, and it feels no pain. The woman jumps to her feet and snatches the lizard out of the pot. See! She drops it right into the middle of the fire. It lies there, hissing and crackling, making no attempt to escape from the searing heat, and its shiny black eyes are fixed on Hutchman's.

I told you so, the woman says. The other soldier goes back to his amorous snuggling, but now Hutchman finds her repulsive. The lizard swells up horribly and bursts – all without struggling to get off the glowing cinders – and the whole time its eyes are staring straight into Hutchman's eyes, reproachfully, intently. It seems to be trying to tell him something. He gets to his feet and runs out of the house, and his horror is mingled with guilt – as though he has betrayed the creature in some way.

But it just lay on the fire, he protests. *It sat there and let itself be burned.*

He lay between the sheets, appalled, for a long time. Fluffy little particles of light drifted down from the sky, floated in through the bedroom window and sought out their assigned positions, gradually re-creating the walls and furniture exactly as they had been yesterday. Vicky was sleeping peacefully close by, but he derived little reassurance from her presence. The ghastly mood of the dream was still upon him, its symbolism baffling and impenetrable, yet creating in his mind a counter-reality in which all the ancient verities no longer stood firm.

All he knew for certain was that he was now committed to building the antibomb machine.

3

While Hutchman was listening to the breakfast-time news Vicky switched the radio off twice, complaining that she had a headache. He got up from the table each time and switched the set on again, but at reduced volume. There was news of sporadic fighting on Syria's borders with Turkey and Iraq, apparently triggered off by sheer frustration on the part of the Syrians, plus multi-layered reports of UN meetings and diplomatic activities in a dozen capitals, statements by obscure liberation fronts, hints at vast fleet movements in the Mediterranean. Hutchman, his senses drowning in the morning sunlight and the welter of domestic immediacy, was able to absorb little of the world situation beyond the fact that as yet no aggressor had been identified. He performed a number of rituals – tying David's shoelaces, taking fresh yoghurt out of the culture box, setting a halibut liver-oil capsule beside each plate – while his mind made the first tentative assessment of what could be involved in actually building the machine.

Producing the maths for a neutron resonator had been one thing, but translating it into functioning hardware was a daunting prospect for a theoretician, especially one depending on private means. The machine was going to cost money. *Real* money – perhaps enough to necessitate mortgaging the house which, ever-present thought, had been given to them by Vicky's father. To start with, all Hutchman had was a frequency corresponding to a fractional-Angstrom wavelength, and the only conceivable way to produce energy at that precise frequency was with a cestron laser.

Problem number one: there were, as far as he knew, no cestron lasers in existence. Cestron was a recently discovered gas, a short-lived product of the praseodymium isotope, and without the guiding star of Hutchman's maths there had been no reason to use it as the basis of a laser. He would have to build one from scratch.

Staring at his son's daydreaming face across the breakfast table, Hutchman felt himself slide into a depressed unease as he considered the practical difficulties. His first requirement was for enough unstable praseodymium to produce, say, fifty millilitres of cestron. He would also need a crystal of praseodymium for use in the laser's exciting circuitry, and the circuits themselves were going to be difficult to build. Hutchman had a little practical experience in electronics, but a machine to handle frequencies in the 6×10^{18} Hertz bracket would employ tubular waveguides in place of wires. *It's going to look more like a piece of plumbing than . . .*

'Lucas!' Vicky tapped his plate with her fork. 'Are you just going to just sit around brooding?'

'I'm not brooding' *. . . and the radiation's going to be hot stuff. More dangerous than X-rays – I'll need shielding – and it'll have to be coupled in to the laser optically. That means buying gold plates and using one of those spinning concave-mirror arrangements to . . .*

'Lucas!' Vicky tugged angrily at his sleeve. 'At least answer David when he speaks to you.'

'I'm sorry.' Hutchman focused his eyes on David who now had his school blazer on and was about to leave. 'Have a good day, son. Did you finish your spellings last night?'

'Nope.' David tightened his lips obstinately, and the face of the man he would one day become momentarily overlaid his features.

'What will you say to the teacher?'

'I'll tell her . . .' David paused for inspiration '. . . to stick her head down the lavatory.' He strode out of the kitchen and a few seconds later they heard him slam the front door as he left for school.

'He tries to sound tough at home, but Miss Lambert tells me he's the quietest boy in his class,' Vicky said.

'That's what worries me. I wonder if he's all that well adjusted to school.'

'David is perfectly adjusted.' Vicky sat down at the table and poured a second cup of coffee, not enquiring if he would like one – a sign that she was annoyed with him. 'You could give him more help with his homework.'

Hutchman shook his head. 'Telling a kid the answers to his homework problems doesn't help him. What I'm doing is teaching him a system of thought which will enable him to solve *any* kind of problem regardless of . . .'

'What does David know about systems of thought?' Vicky's voice was scornful.

'Nothing,' Hutchman said reasonably. 'That's why I'm teaching him.' He felt a flicker of malicious pleasure as Vicky compressed her lips and half-turned away from him to increase the volume on the radio. On an average of once a week he cut her short in an argument by the simple, though logically irrelevant, expedient of answering a rhetorical question as though it had been posed seriously. Vicky never rephrased the question. He suspected this was merely because she had an instinctive contempt for formalism, but its effect was roughly equivalent to a conclusive victory on his part. Now that Vicky had chosen to listen to the radio she seemed to be shutting him out, addressing all her being to it. The morning sun reflected upward from the floor permeating her dressing gown with light, making the flesh of exposed breast and thigh creamy and powdery and translucent. *A good morning for going back to bed for an hour,* Hutchman thought, but there was a sensation of guilt. The vision of Vicky and himself on the lush, soundless divan was bleached into the mural of broken bodies which flared behind his eyes. *How many indomitable seven-year-olds had died in Damascus? And how many . . . ?*

'Oh, Christ!' Vicky switched the radio off with a violent flourish. 'Did you hear that?'

'No.'

'Some pop singer has burned down his house in Virginia Water – as a protest.'

'A protest?' Hutchman spoke absent-mindedly. It had just occurred to him that he was going to need a gas centrifuge to purify the cestron sufficiently for use in a laser.

'With full press and television coverage, of course. How much do you think the publicity will be worth to him?'

'Perhaps he wasn't looking at it that way.'

'Perhaps my ass,' she said with uninspired coarseness. 'You don't understand the whole "Be a millionaire for peace" philosophy, Lucas. The thing, is to do exactly what you want to do, gratify every dirty or selfish little desire you have, but proclaim loudly that you're doing it for peace. That way you can have a hell of a good time and still feel morally superior.'

'There's no point getting into a state about it.' Hutchman was suddenly impatient to get into the office and start going through Westfield's catalogue library. He should also be able to get advice from someone in the purchasing department.

'I can't stand hypocrisy,' Hutchman said incautiously, his thoughts now wholly centred on the antibomb machine.

'What do you mean?'

Hutchman saw the danger of suggesting that his wife was jealous rather than indignant. 'Nothing. Just playing with words.' He swallowed the cold remainder of his coffee, not because he wanted it, but to indicate that he was in a hurry to go to work.

Walking through the Westfield research building towards his office, he saw the first indications that the annihilation of a crowded city had made some kind of mark on everyday life. A few of the smaller offices and cubicles were empty, and others were unusually populated as staff got together to discuss the newscasts. There was an atmosphere of tension, heightened rather than relieved by occasional bursts of defiant laughter. Hutchman was strangely reassured. He knew perfectly well that Vicky was capable of concern for other human beings – more than once she had fled from the room in tears when surprised by the face of a murdered child on the television screen – but her determined, pragmatical insularity of the previous evening had frightened him. That, perhaps, was what the dream had been about. A woman, a womb-carrier, a life-source, looking at death with coolly disinterested eyes.

Muriel Burnley arrived at his office at the same time as Hutchman. She was carrying the straw basket which served her in place of a handbag, and under her arm was a roll of paper which looked like yet another travel poster for her office.

'Good morning, Mr Hutchman,' she said watchfully, the verbal equivalent of moving pawn to king four in the day's new battle.

'Morning, Muriel.' Without quite understanding it, Hutchman could sense the importance Muriel attached to the daily exchange of formal greetings and he had never risked not responding. He opened the door to her office, followed her into the claustrophobic cave, and picked up the small sheaf of mail from her desk. Muriel slipped out of her brown tweed coat, a movement which involved a zooming upward of her incongruously large bosom. Hutchman averted his eyes – knowing she was studying him from behind her brown lenses – and riffled through the mail.

'There's nothing very pressing here,' he said. 'Take care of it for me, will you? Use your own judgment. I'm going to be busy today and I don't want any interruptions.'

Muriel sniffed disapprovingly and took the bunch of envelopes from him. He went into his own office, closed the connecting door carefully, and after a few moments' thought rang Cliff Taylor, Westfield's chief of electronic development. Taylor sounded both surprised and sleepy, but he made no complaint about being called so early in the morning.

'What can I do for you, Hutch?'

'Ah . . . well, I'm trying out something involving microwave radiation and I want to do the breadboard work myself. I wondered if you could give me the use of a room for a month or so.'

'I don't know, Hutch. We've got all kinds of requirements being thrown at us on the Jack-and-Jill programme . . . Is it important?'

'Very.' Hutchman traced a large D on the glassy surface of his desk. D for death. Big D used to mean Dallas and death, now it means Damascus and . . .

'Well, why don't you get Mackeson to slap a few priority points on it to satisfy the computer gang?'

'It's a semiprivate job, Cliff. Could be valuable to Westfield eventually, but I want to keep it to myself in case the whole thing fizzles out into nothing. I couldn't go to Mackeson.'

'Can't help you then. I mean . . . what sort of facilities did you want?' Taylor was beginning to sound querulous, apparently sensing that Hutchman was being dishonest with him.

'Nothing much. A bench in a room I can lock up. The power supplies don't even have to be stabilized.'

'Just a minute, Hutch. You said microwave a minute ago. How micro is micro?'

'Pretty micro.' Hutchman could feel the conversation getting out of hand – the very first person to whom he had mentioned what would have to be the world's most secret project was becoming suspicious and asking pertinent questions. 'Maybe 6×10^{18} Hertz.'

'Christ! That kills it altogether. The zoning regulations don't allow us to squirt that sort of radiation around unless we have all kinds of special shielding installed in the building. Sorry, Hutch.'

'It's all right.' Hutchman put the phone down and sat staring at the frosted-glass partition and the moving grey blur which meant that Don Spain had arrived in the office earlier than usual. The project was going as he might have predicted, following the same pattern as his previous brushes with physical reality – at the lowest level – the 'ten-minute' car repair jobs in which, after a full hour, he was still struggling to budge the first nut. Some people had the blessed knack of controlling their circumstances and mastering materials – others, like Hutchman, had to be content with building beautiful edifices in logic, knowing all the while they were incapable of translating them into actuality. His throat was constricting with helpless rage when the internal phone rang. He snatched it before Muriel could pick up the extension.

'Hello, Hutch.' It was Taylor again. 'I've been thinking around your problem. Did you know that Westfield's have the use of a lab in the Jeavons Institute over at Camburn?'

'I'd heard about it, vaguely.' Hutchman's heart began a steady, peaceful pounding.

'It's a fairly informal arrangement we fixed up about the time they got old man Westfield to outfit their cryogenics suite. What it boils down to is that we have the use of the lab when they aren't pushed for space.'

'And what's the situation now?'

'As far as I know they'll be pretty well marking time till after Christmas. If you like I'll ring Professor Duering and see if I can fix it for you to go over there.'

'I'd be grateful if you would, Cliff.' Hutchman, choking on a tide of warm thankfulness, had difficulty getting the words out in a normal tone. When he set the phone down he experienced a heady moment of certitude. He left his office and hurried upstairs to the purchasing department, where he spent more than two hours making notes in the catalogue library and checking on the availability of major items. In the afternoon he got confirmation from Taylor that the Jeavons Institute Laboratory was available, and drove over to look at it and collect the keys from Duering. By five o'clock, his normal quitting time, he had not done a single stroke of work on behalf of Westfield's, but he was ready to begin drawing detailed schematics for the antibomb machine. He got Muriel to order him a pot of tea as she was leaving, and, as the building fell silent for the weekend, settled in to preparing the first drawings.

An hour later, when his concentration was at its height, he became aware of a sudden unease, a sense that something was wrong. His mind had sunk too deeply into the complex of lines and symbols to be easily distracted, but part of him began to keep guard, to spread its network of perception. *There's trouble. That grey object which Muriel has left lying against the partition on her side*

41

looks like a face. That's what's been making me feel jumpy. Hutchman lifted his pocket computer and was adjusting the cursor when his eyes focused on the grey object. Its cloudy features stared back impassively.

It is a face!

He started convulsively as he realized he was being observed through the frosty glass, then came the secondary realization that it had to be Don Spain. The accountant must also have been working late, but the unnatural silence which had made Hutchman unaware of his presence for an hour could only have been achieved by intent. With cool ripples of shock still coursing through his system, Hutchman casually slid his sheets of graph paper into a folder and covered it with his blotter. Spain's face remained motionless at the partition. Hutchman took a small pencil sharpener from a drawer and threw it hard at the ghostly face. It struck the partition with a sharp crack, almost splintering the glass, and Spain disappeared from view. A few seconds later he opened the connecting door and entered from Muriel's office.

'What's the idea, Hutch?' he asked indignantly. 'You might have smashed that glass into my face.'

'What the hell's the idea of standing out there staring at me?'

'I didn't know you were here. I was working late and I thought I heard a noise in your office so I came out to see what it was.'

'Thanks,' Hutchman said heavily, making no attempt to conceal his dislike of the other man. 'It didn't occur to you to open the door?'

'I didn't want to burst in on you. After all . . .' Spain chuckled throatily '. . . you might have had a woman in here.'

'That's the first thought that popped into your mind, is it?'

Spain shrugged and continued to grin. 'It isn't like you to work late, Hutch, and you've been acting a bit strange all day. Those symptoms are all part of the Batterbee syndrome. You remember Batterbee, don't you?'

Hutchman nodded as his dread of Spain returned in full force. Batterbee had been a senior project engineer, much celebrated in Westfield lore, who had lost his job through being caught in *flagrante delicto* with his secretary on the office carpet while supposed to be working overtime. Spain never tired of retelling the story.

'Sorry to disappoint you,' Hutchman said. He picked up his pencil and made a show of jotting figures on his notepad, but Spain stayed around for a further fifteen minutes discussing office politics. By the time he left Hutchman's ability to concentrate had been seriously impaired and he had begun to feel tired. He forced himself to work on, intending to have the schematics worked out before going to bed so that in the morning he could concentrate on the problems of buying hardware. It was past nine when he crammed all the paperwork into his briefcase and went out into the darkness. The soft, thick October air was filled with the smell of decaying chestnut leaves and a brilliant planet shone low in the western sky, like a coachlamp. He breathed deeply while walking to his car – inhale for four paces, hold for four paces, exhale for four paces – and waved goodnight to the officer in the security kiosk at the main gate. It was a pleasant night, providing one didn't think too deeply about man-made suns in brief blossom over defenceless cities.

The Home Counties evening traffic was at its incredible worst and at one point, where he should have made a right turn onto the Crymchurch road, he had to turn left and make a twenty-minute detour with the result that he did not reach home until well past ten o'clock. The house was ablaze with light behind its screen of poplars, as though a party were in progress, but there was utter silence when he went in through the side door from the carport. He found Vicky scanning a magazine in the lounge and one glance at her white, set face reminded him that he had omitted to telephone and let her know he would be late. A standard lamp close behind her chair cast a cone of apricot-coloured light in which the magazine's turning pages flared briefly.

'Sorry,' he said, setting his briefcase on a chair. 'I was working late at the office.'

Vicky flipped two pages before replying 'Is that what you call it?'

'I do call working, working; late, late; and the office, the office,' Hutchman said tartly. 'Which particular word are you having difficulty with?'

Vicky nodded silently, continuing to flick through the magazine. This was the phase of an argument in which Hutchman usually did well because his wife disdained word-spinning. Later on, when the rapiers were broken and the cudgels came out, she would gain the upper hand, but it would be the small hours of morning before that stage was reached, and there would be very little sleep for either of them. The prospect of another tortured night filled Hutchman with helpless anger.

He stood in front of Vicky and addressed the top of her head. 'Listen, Vicky, you don't *really* think I've been with another woman, do you?'

She tilted her gaze to meet his, a look of polite surprise on the small desperate face. 'I didn't mention another woman, Lucas. Why did you?'

'Because you were about to.'

'Don't let your conscience put words into my mouth.' Vicky reached the end of the magazine, turned it over, and began flicking pages at precisely the same rate as before.

'I haven't *got* a conscience.'

'I know that. What's her name, Lucas? Was it Maudie Werner?'

'Who's Maudie Werner, for God's sake?'

'The new . . . tart in data processing.'

Hutchman turned without speaking and went into the kitchen, the struggle to control his nerves making the act of walking seem difficult. He took some cold chicken and a carton of Russian salad from the refrigerator and put them on a plate.

It's happened again, he thought. *Like telepathy. Spain's mind and Vicky's working in exactly the same way, on exactly the same subterranean level.* He salted the chicken, took a fork from a drawer, and went back into the lounge.

'Tell me, Vicky,' he said, 'am I some kind of a sexual simpleton? When I leave a room do the men and women in it leap at each other and frig like rabbits till they hear me returning?'

'What are you talking about?'

'About the impression I sometimes get from you and one or two other people.'

'And you,' Vicky said scathingly, 'try to tell me that *I'm* crazy!'

Even when his wife had finally gone to sleep, Hutchman lay in the darkness for a long time listening to the invisible tides of night air flow around and through the house. His mind was racing, taking fragments of the day – glossy catalogues heavy with a smell like that of fresh paint, the complex schematics drawn by hand, Spain's blurred face staring, the evening news of mobilizations and fleet movements, Vicky's neurotic jealousy – assembling them in fantastic composites of foreboding which dissolved and reformed into new patterns of menace. Sleep came suddenly, bringing with it another dream, in which he was shopping in a supermarket. A frozen-food bin was close by and two women were examining its contents.

'I like this new idea,' one of them said. She reached into the bin and lifted out a white spiky object, like a skinless and terribly misshapen fish. It had two sad grey eyes. 'It's the latest thing in food preservation. They give it a pseudo-life which maintains it in perfect condition till it's ready for the pan.'

The other woman looked alarmed. 'Isn't that cruel?'

'No. It has no soul, and it feels no pain.' To prove her point, she began snapping off the white fleshy extrusions and dropping them into her basket. Hutchman backed away from the scene in horror, because, although the fish-thing lay motionless and allowed itself to be demolished, its eyes were fixed on his – calmly, sadly, reproachfully.

4

October – the entire span of which was occupied by the building of the machine – was a difficult road, in Hutchman's mind. It was a road measured by double-sided milestones showing both the decreasing distance to the project's completion and the ever-widening gulf over which he and Vicky viewed each other.

One of the first had been the day on which he had acquired the praseodymium crystal and enough of the green isotope to produce the necessary fifty milligrams of cestron in a reasonable time. He had gone straight from work to the refectory at the Jeavons and eaten a quick snack, avoiding conversation with others even though he had a feeling that a dark-haired woman several tables away had been known to him in the past. That night he had worked later than usual to set up the gas-collecting system, and on reaching home had found himself locked out.

This can't be happening to me! Hutchman shook his head in disbelief, but his key was unable to turn the lock of the front door and the side entrance was securely bolted against him. He paused, staring down at his silhouette on the moonlit path, one part of his mind sliding into irrelevant thoughts as to why the shadow cast by the moon made his head seem smaller than in the shadow cast by a streetlight. The house was dark and silent, robbed of its familiarity by circumstance. It suddenly came to him what a shocking thing it would be if he, Lucas Hutchman, were forced to stay outside all night. Even more appalling was the discovery of how effective the childishness of one adult can be against the reasonableness of another. He tried all the windows in vain then returned to the main bedroom window and began tapping the glass. As the minutes went by with no response his self-control began to fail and he drove his fist harder and harder, hoping the pane would shatter.

'Vicky!' He called her name in a fierce low chant. 'Vicky! Vicky!'

The lock clicked loudly on the front door. He ran to it eagerly, yet half-afraid of what he might do to Vicky with the clublike objects his fists had become, and found David peering at him with the eyes of a tarsier.

'Sorry, son. I got locked out.' Hutchman lifted the pyjama-clad child and carried him into the house, closing the door with his heel. He put David into bed then went into the main bedroom where Vicky was lying perfectly still, pretending to be asleep. The thought of being able to lay his cold, weary body down beside her, and of not having to stay outside in the ancient England of runes and robbers which seemed to re-create itself in the darkness, drained away his anger. He undressed quickly, got in between the sheets, and slid his arm around the familiar torso. On the instant, Vicky was out of bed and standing at the far side of the room, her naked body voluptuously shaded by the moonlight.

'Don't touch me.' Her voice fractured, like ice.

He sat up. 'Vicky, what's the matter?'

'Just don't try to touch me. I'll sleep in the other room.'

'Why are you behaving like this?' Hutchman spoke carefully, aware of how much was in the balance. He knew perfectly well what the uncomfortable little tableau was all about – memories of previous walks through this section of the Marriage Exhibition came shimmering. *How dare you suggest there's anything wrong with my*

48

mind! Is a woman insane if she doesn't want a filthy disease brought into the house, to her and her child? The trouble was he could not say he knew what was in her mind because – Vicky fought like a retiarius, always spreading her net in the same way while poising the trident – she would turn it into an admission of guilt.

'You will not sleep in the other room,' he said firmly.

'I'm not sleeping in that bed. Not *now*.'

Not now that it could be contaminated with his filthy disease, Hutchman interpreted, seeing the net swirl towards him again. He evaded it by saying nothing. Instead he got out of bed and moved towards her. Vicky vanished through the bedroom door, and it took him a second to realize she had turned right towards the front door. He followed her into the short corridor as the main door opened to admit a gust of night air which probed insouciantly around his unprotected body. Vicky was outside, standing in the centre of the lawn.

'Don't touch me,' she shouted. 'I'd rather stay out here all night.'

'Oh, Jesus,' Hutchman said aloud, but not addressing anyone. 'What am I going to do?' Vicky could run well, so there was little hope of his catching her even if he decided to give chase and risk attracting the attention of outsiders. He turned back into the house, leaving the door open, and walked slowly into the second bedroom. Sometime later he heard the front door closing and there came a momentary hope, dismaying in its intensity, that Vicky would come to him with dew-cold breasts and thighs, seeking warmth. But she went into the other room, leaving him huddled in his bitterness.

Attempting an explanation would have been disastrous whether it was believed or rejected. Either way, Vicky would talk – to her parents, to her friends and neighbours,

49

to his colleagues – and that would be dangerous, because people would remember the things she said. The short-term goal of completing the machine was filling his mind, but beyond it the first outlines of a plan were taking shape. Vague though it was, one element was apparent – the frightful danger to himself, his wife, and even David. The machine had to be built in secret, yet before it would serve its purpose the secret would have to be broken thoroughly and systematically in a process which Hutchman could initiate but would find difficult to control. And Vicky, whom he had never been able to control, had to be kept in utter ignorance, even while stress patterns rippled through the structure of their marriage, building up in holographic concentrations around critical points such as the second milestone.

A gas centrifuge, in perfect condition but at a price he could afford, had become available in Manchester. Hutchman drove up and collected it with the intention of being back in Crymchurch by late evening, but the Midlands were submerged in fog. He got no further south than Derby before news of a multiple crash with fatalities at Belper prompted him to seek out a motel. It was almost midnight when he called Vicky to let her know he would not be home. The phone rang blurrily, as though the moisture-laden air was slowly drowning all things electronic and mechanical, and there was no reply. Hutchman was not particularly surprised. Vicky would have a fair idea of who was ringing, and why, so by not answering she was putting him at a disadvantage.

He set the phone down and stretched himself fully clothed on the chalet's neat bed. That morning he had told Vicky the simple truth about his visit to Manchester, knowing her mind would shy away from the technicalities involved, and had asked her to come with him. She had said that he *knew* she would not keep David away from

50

school for the day, and her tone implied that he would not have offered to take her with him otherwise. One up to Vicky. *The damned machine,* he thought. *It's costing me too much. Who do I think I am, anyway?* Sixteen days had elapsed since the bomb had exploded on Damascus and as yet nobody had accepted the blame or, to put it another way, been able to do enough violence to the framework of political morality to make the action seem creditable, or even expedient. The Middle Eastern situation appeared paradoxically more stable than at any time since Syria's abrupt withdrawal from the Arab Union – and Hutchman was faced with the fact that his machine would not bring any indomitable seven-year-olds back to life. It was a thought which, in the throbbing emptiness of the alien room, seemed worthy of consideration.

He reached Crymchurch in mid-morning and found the house locked up and empty. Milk bottles were on the doorstep and several items of mail were lying on the hall floor. He knew at once that Vicky and David had left sometime during the previous day. Suppressing a surge of self-pity which closed up his throat, he picked up the telephone, and began to ring Vicky's parents, then changed his mind. She had run emotionally naked to her parents and, as on the night she had fled out onto the lawn, the best way to bring her back was to leave the door open and wait.

Three days went by before Vicky returned on a rainy Saturday morning, looking contrite and a little shame-faced, accompanied by her parents. Her father, Alderman James Morris, white-haired and strawberry-nosed, spoke long and seriously to Hutchman about things like the cost of electricity and the uncertain nature of the money market. He never once mentioned his daughter's marriage or expressed any views on what might be wrong with it, but the gravity of his tones seemed to convey a message outside their content. Hutchman answered all his remarks with equal seriousness. As soon as Vicky's parents had left he sought her out in the bedroom. She smiled tearfully and pressed her palms downward against her hips like a little girl hoping for leniency after a prank, an action which spread her tawny shoulders within the oatmeal-coloured satin of her blouse.

'Where's David?' he demanded.

'He was still in bed when I left. Dad's taking him to the planetarium this afternoon and bringing him over later.'

'Oh!' Hutchman could feel sexuality pulsing in the quiet air. It was almost three weeks since they had made love and now, suddenly, glandular pressures were causing real pain.

'It was all a holiday for him, Lucas.'

'And for you?'

'I . . .' She came to him open-mouthed and hungry, and during the following hours she handled him with special tenderness until all the pain had left his body. Hutchman lay listening to the rain on the bedroom windows, the sane sound of rain, and wondered guiltily how Vicky would react when she learned that this time the pattern was going to be different. In the saw-tooth graph of their relationship a reconciliation scene was always followed by an idyllic period of harmony – but there had never been The Peace Machine to consider.

'It's a private research project into some properties of microwave radiation.' The 'explanation' baffled Vicky, as he intended it to, and the more he repeated it the greater her bewilderment became. She was forced to accept the reality of the project but, without any hint of the incredible truth behind it, could only conjecture about Hutchman's involvement. Others too, in spite of all his efforts, were noticing the changes. He had fallen behind in his work – a fact increasingly apparent at the weekly Jack-and-Jill progress meetings. Muriel Burnley went about her secretarial duties with open watchfulness, showing her resentment in a hundred irritating ways, and Don Spain was both fevered and elated with his certainty that Hutchman was up to his neck in a disastrous affair.

Hutchman worked steadily on the project, at times unable to believe the degree to which he was committed, spending as much time at the Jeavons Institute as he dared, and at the same time trying not to imperil the slight improvement in his relations with Vicky. At the end of the month he had an operational cestron laser, and had reached yet another major milestone.

'What does this mean?' Vicky spun the letter across the breakfast table.

Even before he picked it up Hutchman recognized the neat, dull heading of his bank. 'This letter was addressed to me,' he said, numbly, trying to gain time to think.

'Who cares about that? What does it *mean*?'

He scanned the professionally terse note which stated that his current account was overdrawn by more than a thousand pounds and that, as he had closed his savings account, the bank would be obliged if he would deposit fresh funds immediately or call to discuss the matter with the manager.

'It means what it says,' he commented. 'We owe the bank some money.'

'But how can we be overdrawn by so much?' Vicky's face was turning white at the corners of her mouth.

'That's what I'd like to know.' It had been a mistake, Hutchman realized, to allow the account to get so far out of hand and an even bigger one to have permitted a letter about it to come to the house.

'And why didn't they simply transfer some cash from

the savings account the way they usually . . .' Vicky snatched the letter back and read it again. 'But you've *closed* the savings account! Where's the money?'

Hutchman tried to sound calm. 'I had to use it – for the project.'

'*What!*' Vicky gave a shaky laugh and glanced at David, who had looked up from his cereal with interest. 'You have to be joking, Lucas – I had over four thousand pounds in that account.'

Hutchman noted her use of the singular pronoun. Vicky was a director in the smallish contracting business owned by her father. She allowed her salary to accumulate in the savings account and studiously referred to it as 'our' savings, except in moments of anger.

'I'm not joking,' Hutchman said. 'I needed it to buy equipment.'

'I don't believe you. What sort of equipment? Show me the receipts.'

'I'll try to find them.' He had bought the equipment on a cash basis, using a fictitious name and address, and then had burned the receipts. Being a dancing master to neutrons involved strange disciplines. 'But I'm not hopeful.' He watched Vicky helplessly as tears began to spill down her cheeks in transparent ribbons.

'I know why you can't show me any receipts,' she said. 'I know the kind of equipment you've been buying.'

Here we go again, Hutchman thought in a panic. Interpreted in the context of all his years with Vicky, her words were a direct accusation that he had squandered the money on a woman or women, perhaps had even bought an apartment for use as a love nest. They both knew what she meant, but – and this was the familiar Vicky battle technique – if he denied that tacit change he would be admitting it.

'Please, Vicky, *please*.' He nodded towards David.

'I've never done anything to harm David,' Vicky assured him. 'But I'll hurt you, Lucas Hutchman. I'll pay you back for this.'

The knowledge that he was not going to use the antibomb machine crystallized slowly in Hutchman's mind as he checked through the intricacies of the final assembly. He wondered for a moment if it had always been present at some level of consciousness, but occulted by his obsession with the project as a project. His hands continued to work and he stared down ruefully as though they had been the sole designers of the machine. Regardless of the thought processes, now that the machine was a reality he was faced with a daunting, multifaceted truth.

One facet was that the machine could not be tested or used on a limited scale. It was an all-or-nothing device, strictly intended for all-or-nothing people – a category to which Hutchman did not really belong. Another facet was that the international situation appeared to have changed for the better. Some observers felt that the air had been cleared a little, that a subconscious but a worldwide yearning to use the bomb had been expunged. Closely related to this was Hutchman's reluctance to go any further along the path which was leading to the end of his marriage. It was difficult for him to accept that he was prepared to stake millions of human lives against his own happiness – if that was the correct way to describe his life with Vicky – but the machine was real, shockingly real, more real than anything he had ever seen before. It overwhelmed him with its three-dimensional presence, leaving no room for illusion or double-think. And the truth he had to accept? *I am, after all, just as selfish, cowardly, and ordinary as anybody else.*

Hutchman put his micrometer aside with a growing sense of relief, tempered with the guilty joy which comes with a lowering of one's standards. Two hours' work was all that was required to finalize the alignments and complete the machine; however, there was no point in it now. He debated dismantling the apparatus there and then, but he had opened the floodgates of weariness which had been building up inside him for a month. His legs began to tremble gently. He surveyed the machine soberly for a moment, making his peace with it, then walked out of the room and locked the door behind him.

Several times on the drive back to Crymchurch he annoyed other drivers by slowing down when there was no external reason for it, but all urgency seemed to have fled from his mind. He wanted to coast, in every sense of the word, to immerse himself in the warm flow of life from which he had so painfully crawled for a time. The mural of broken bodies had ceased to pulse in his vision, and once again he was *ordinary*. Great sighs interspersed themselves with his normal breathing as he drove on through the darkness, and he had a sense of being at an important turning point in life. Massive doors seemed to be clanging into place, sealing off dangerous avenues of probability.

Hutchman was disappointed to find an unfamiliar car parked in his driveway. It was a two-seater coupe, plum-coloured or brown – it was difficult to decide in the dim light from the house, and part of his mind noted irrelevantly that it was parked with its nose towards the gate, as though the owner had given thought to leaving with the minimum delay. If there was a stranger in the house he would not be free to tell Vicky the things he wanted to tell her. Frowning, Hutchman put his key in the front-door lock and twisted it, but the key refused to turn. The Yale mechanism was double-locked on the inside.

Hutchman stepped back from the porch, examined the

house, and saw that the only light was a faint glow from David's bedroom window. A visitor in the house but no lights on? The enormity of the idea which came to him caused Hutchman to move quietly to the side door and try to get in. It, too, was double-locked. He ran back to the front door and now the lounge lights were on. He hit the door with his fist and pounded steadily on it until the lock clicked. Vicky was standing there, wearing a blue-silk kimono.

'What do you think you're doing?' she demanded coldly. 'David's asleep.'

'Why were the lights out and the doors locked?'

'Who said the lights were out?' Vicky continued to stand in the opening, as if refusing him admittance. 'And why are you home so early?'

Hutchman walked straight at his wife, ignoring her startled gasp, and threw open the door of the lounge. A tanned, dark-haired man of about forty, whom Hutchman identified vaguely as the owner of the local service station, was standing in the centre of the room. He was pulling his trousers up over black-satin briefs and his shocked face, above the weight-trained torso, was – an image flashed into Hutchman's chilled brain – that of Lee Harvey Oswald just as Ruby's bullet hit him.

'You!' Hutchman snapped, his mind still working with unexpected cryogenic efficiency. 'Get dressed and get out of here.' He watched the other man slip into his shirt, noting that even in a moment of presumed stress he did so in the classical locker-room manner, one leg slightly bent, abdominal muscles tightly contracted to present a flattering posture.

'This is unforgivable,' Vicky breathed. 'How dare you spy on me, then speak to my guest like that!'

'Your *guest* isn't objecting. Are you, guest?'

The heavily built man stepped into his shoes and lifted his jacket from a chair without speaking.

'This is my house, Forest,' Vicky said to him, 'and you don't have to leave. In fact, I'm asking you right now not to leave.'

'Well . . .' Forest looked at Hutchman, the bafflement slowly fading from his eyes to be replaced by a tentative belligerency. He flexed his shoulder muscles like a cobra spreading its hood.

'Dear me,' Hutchman said with affected weariness. He stepped backwards into the hall, lifted a three-foot machete from its hooks on the wall, and returned to the lounge. 'Listen to me, Forest. I'm not angry with you about what happened here earlier – you simply happened to be walking by when the fruit machine paid off – but now you're intruding on my privacy and if you don't go away from here I mean to kill you.'

'Don't believe him,' Vicky laughed shakily and moved closer to Forest.

Hutchman glanced around the room, picked out a Hepplewhite chair which Vicky's father had given to her the previous year, and split its shield-shaped back in two with the machete. Vicky gave a low scream but the act of vandalism seemed to have proved something to Forest, who headed determinedly for the front door. She followed him for a few paces, then abruptly appeared to lose interest.

'Destroying that chair wasn't very bright,' she said disinterestedly. 'It was worth money.'

Hutchman waited till the car outside had started up and moved away before he spoke. 'Just tell me one thing. Was this the first night your . . . guest was here?'

'No, Lucas.' Vicky's voice was incongruously tender, unmanning him. 'This wasn't the first night.'

'Then . . .' Now that there was no outsider present for

Hutchman to play to he was, for the second time in an hour, confronted with reality. He grasped its white-hot metal. 'Then I was too late.'

'Much too late.' Again the cruel tenderness.

'I wish I could make you see how wrong you've been, Vicky. I've never been unfaithful to you. I . . .' Hutchman stopped speaking as his throat closed in pain. *All these years,* he thought. *All the beautiful, flawed years thrown away. And for what?*

'You started this, Lucas. At least be man enough to go through with it without crying.' Vicky lit a cigarette as she spoke, her eyes hard and triumphant behind a writhing mask of smoke.

'All right, Vicky,' he managed to say, and for a moment he could almost see the antibomb machine interposed between them. 'I promise I'll go through with it.'

5

'If you have something on your mind, domestic or otherwise, which is affecting your work – why don't you tell me about it?' Arthur Boswell, head of missile research and development at Westfield's, put on his gold-rimmed spectacles and looked closely at Hutchman. His eyes were very blue and very inquisitive behind their flakes of glass.

'There isn't any special problem, Arthur.' Hutchman faced the older man across an expanse of rosewood desk and wondered if he should have admitted to some kind of a personal crisis if only to make the next few days in the office a little easier.

'I see.' Boswell let his gaze travel nostalgically around the big office, with its twenty-year-old photographs of missile firings on the panelled walls. 'You haven't been looking at all well, lately, Hutch.'

'Ah . . . no.' Hutchman too glanced around the office, wishing he could think of something useful to say, but his mind kept dwelling on the idea that missile photographs were incongruous in the atmosphere with which Boswell was trying to surround himself. They should have been brown prints of stick-and-string aircraft, dating from Asquith and Lloyd George, with fragile, organic-looking wings. 'As a matter of fact, I haven't been sleeping properly for some time. I suppose I ought to see the quack and get some pills.'

'Sleep's important. You can't manage for long without it,' Boswell pronounced. 'Why can't you sleep?'

'No special reason.' *Back to square one,* Hutchman thought. *Arthur has something on his mind.*

'I'm considering giving you an assistant, Hutch.'

'There's no need for that,' Hutchman said in sudden alarm – the last thing he wanted was a stranger billeted in his office. 'I mean there's no point in it. I'll be through the work in a couple of weeks and it would take a new man that long to brief himself properly.'

'Two weeks,' Boswell appeared to seize on the definite statement. 'We couldn't give it much more. The board want to reach a definite decision about Jack and Jill next month.'

'Two weeks is all I need,' Hutchman assured him. He left Boswell's office with the self-imposed deadline singing in his ears and hurried upstairs to the less sumptuous environs in which most of the R and D staff worked. Two weeks would be just about enough time in which to make the world's nuclear powers aware of the existence of his machine provided he worked quickly and made no wrong moves. *I will work quickly, Vicky, and I'll make no mistakes. Just for you.*

A task he had to get on with immediately was writing out a summary of his maths and a specification for the machine. These would have to be copied several hundred times then mailed out to a list of institutions and individuals across the world. A minor difficulty was that the mailings would have to be scheduled to allow for varying delivery times to different countries, so that all would reach their destinations at roughly the same time. And a major difficulty was that as soon as the envelopes were opened, a lot of people – powerful, ruthless people – would want Hutchman killed. The only way to forestall them, he realized, would be to maintain a high degree of secrecy. Up till now he had assumed that the secure drawer of his desk was a safe enough place to keep his original notes and schematics, but there were those in the company who considered Westfield's security an elaborate joke. Hand all our secret plans to the Russians, the saying went, then they'll be five years behind *us*.

A prey to fresh unease, Hutchman discovered he could not even remember locking the drawer. He speeded up his pace until he was almost running along the corridor, and burst into his office. Don Spain was standing at Hutchman's desk, his grey-jowled face intent as he riffled through the papers in the secure drawer.

'Ho there, Hutch,' he said hoarsely, grinning. 'Where do you keep your pencil sharpener?'

'Not in there,' Hutchman snapped, and almost as an after-thought added, 'You prying little bastard.'

Spain's grin disappeared. 'What's the matter with you, Hutch? I was only trying to borrow a sharpener.'

Hutchman went to the inner door to Muriel's office and slammed it shut. 'That's a lie,' he stated flatly. 'And the reason I know it's a lie is that you've been though my desk so many times you could find the sharpener in the dark. No, Spain, the truth of the matter is that you're a creepy, prying little bastard.'

Brick-coloured smudges appeared in the grey of Spain's face, followed by one of anger. 'Don't get carried away, Hutch. I've no interest in your bloody scrawls, and I'm not going to let a big drink of water like you talk to me as . . .'

Lifting the varnished pebble paperweight from his desk, Hutchman made as if to throw it. Spain ducked aside with comic agility and vanished into Muriel's office. Hutchman sat down at his desk and waited for his nerves to settle. He had wanted to do that for years, but perhaps it would have been better to hold himself in check a little longer. His little display would be widely reported by Spain and Muriel throughout Westfield's just at a time when he wanted to blend into the background.

He inspected the secure drawer and was relieved to

find that his mailing list of government departments, politicians, and influential scientists was close to the bottom and folded in such a way that Spain would probably have passed it by. From now on he would keep all his paperwork on his person, but what about the machine itself?

Hutchman slumped in his chair and stared through the office windows, scored diagonally by occasional raindrops, at autumn-coloured trees. The machine, which was barely portable, could not stay at the Jeavons. To blackmail the nuclear powers, to convert megadeaths to megalives, he would have to set the machine up in a secret place. It would not matter if it was traced eventually, because his would only be the first – once the knowledge of how to build it was disseminated others would be produced from time to time, in hidden rooms. And nobody would be able to risk owning baubles of grey metal. *Ever again, Vicky. Ever again.*

Hutchman stood up and regarded his image in the glass partition, allowing himself a moment of paranoiac indulgence. The shadow man he was looking at, the tall figure with sculptured black hair and long dry hands thrown into prominence by a stray beam of light, was the Lucas Hutchman the rest of the world saw. That Lucas Hutchman – *keep on referring to yourself in the third person, Hutch, classical symptom* – was going to take on the whole world single-handed. And one day that man's wife would understand, finally, when it was too late. And that man's wife would know her own guilt.

Disturbed at the pleasure the game gave him, Hutchman sat down abruptly and shuffled through his notes and sketches. They were all done on Westfield graph paper but that could be rendered anonymous by trimming the name from the top. The trouble was that his scribbles might be impossible for a foreigner to decipher – and it would be better if his handwriting did not appear any-where in the folio. He went into Muriel's claustrophobic office and, ignoring her wary gaze, took a sheaf of plain copy paper from her desk without speaking. It took him almost an hour to write out the entire maths for a neutron resonator and to detail his version of the hardware, using block letters throughout.

As soon as the job was finished he put the paperwork into his briefcase, and began to think about a suitable hiding place for the machine. Somewhere along the south coast, perhaps? He looked at the classified phone directory, found six names of estate agents in Crym-church, and began calling them in alphabetical order. The second one was able to offer him a cottage in Hastings. Hutchman reached for his scrap pad to write down the address and discovered he had left it on his bookcase. He swore impatiently, then jotted the infor-mation on the side of a new green eraser.

'This sounds as though it could be just what I'm looking for,' he told the girl at the other end of the line. 'I'll call at your office later today.'

He told Muriel, by way of the intercom, that he was going out on private business for an hour, and took his briefcase out to his car. It was warm for November but a despairing sky was sagging between the tops of the trees and buildings, and rain was falling with the quiet assurance that it would continue for the rest of the day. As he drove into Crymchurch water droplets crawled along the side-windows like frantic amoebae. Hutch-man parked in the town centre then went to an office-equipment supplier and bought a used copying machine and a supply of paper for £60. He paid in cash, using the money Vicky had given him to replenish their current account, and avoided giving his name. With the copier stowed in the back of his car he walked slowly along the glistening main street looking for the office of the estate agent he had telephoned. It was the third he reached and in the window was a photograph of the house. It was a terrace house, to rent on a winter-only basis. Hutchman estimated that Hastings was about sixty miles away – a ninety-minute drive – which would be about right for his purpose. It was convenient enough to let him install the machine there without suspicious absences from home, yet far enough away so that he could hide efficiently when the time came. He went into the agent's office and in less than half an hour had rented the house until the beginning of April, claiming he was a writer who wanted to get away in solitude to complete a book. He gave a false name, paid the full rental in advance by cash, and came out with two new keys and the unfamiliar address written on a scrap of paper in his pocket.

His next call was at Woolworth's, where he bought several hundred cheap envelopes of a kind which were on sale all over the country. At the general post office he bought sheets of airmail and inland stamps, and put them into his briefcase. A check on the time showed him it was close to his lunch hour so he went into one of his favourite inns in Crymchurch. Joe's was a dismal little place which scorned the midday soup-and-coffee trade but supplied hot Irish whiskey exactly the way he liked it. Seated in a dim corner, with the aromatic drink at hand, he took a sheet of paper from his case and began to compose a letter.

He started with the words, 'To whom it may concern.' They were dismayingly unoriginal, but Hutchman considered them relevant. He had two more whiskies while finishing the draft letter, then read it over.

'This letter is the most important that you will ever read.

'Its contents are of supreme importance to the security

of your country, and to the welfare of the entire human race.

'When you have read it you will be personally responsible for ensuring that the proper steps are taken.

'Your own conscience must decide what those steps are.

'The documents accompanying this letter are:

'a. A mathematical proof that it is possible to build a neutron resonator based on a cestron laser. The radiation will be self-propagating and will have the effect of artificially stimulating neutron flux in all concentrations of fissionable material approaching critical mass. In other words, *activation of the device will cause virtually instantaneous detonation of every nuclear bomb on this planet!*

'b. A schematic showing one simple form of neutron resonator which can be built in a matter of days.

'*Read the following paragraph carefully:*

'THIS MACHINE IS ALREADY IN EXISTENCE. IT WILL BE ACTIVATED AT NOON GMT ON 10TH NOVEMBER 1988. YOU MUST NOW ACT ACCORDINGLY!'

To Hutchman's critical gaze, the letter was reminiscent of one of the injunctions he often received from book clubs, but he was satisfied that it would serve its purpose. All the salesmanship that was required would be carried out on his behalf by the closely written pages of maths. They would present his credentials to every member of the world fraternity of mathematicians who were capable of working on that plane, who would in turn influence others, who would in turn . . . The letter itself, he realized suddenly, was a form of neutron resonator. One which would produce a chain reaction on the human level.

Arranging a hiding place for the machine had been easier and quicker than he had expected, creating a feeling that everything was moving along with supernatural smoothness. On impulse, Hutchman went to the public telephone in a whitewashed alcove at the rear of the inn, rang Westfield's, and got through to Muriel. Her voice was blurred and he guessed her mouth was full of the chocolate wafers she invariably ate at lunchtime in the company of other secretaries who gathered in her office to discuss pop singers.

'Sorry to interupt the proceedings at Culture Corner,' he said, 'I just wanted to let you know I won't be back in the office today. Handle anything that crops up, will you?'

'Where will I say you are?' Her voice was clearer now, but resentful.

'Say I'm at the seaside.' He thought of the red-brown beach at Hastings and wished he had not mentioned the seaside. 'No, you'd better tell the truth – I'll be doing some research at the Morrison Library.'

'Doing some research at the Morrison Library,' Muriel repeated in a dull monotone which openly signalled her disbelief. By this time a suitably edited version of his row with Spain would be going the rounds and Muriel, although she disliked Spain, would have seized on it as another example of how Mr Hutchman had changed for the worse. It occurred to him that he had better be more careful with Muriel.

'That's it,' he said. 'See you in the morning.'

She hung up without replying. He hurried back to his car and drove through the afternoon greyness to the Jeavons Institute. The stone building was vapouring introspectively in the rain and nobody appeared to notice as he parked in the inner quadrangle. It took him twenty minutes to separate the machine into its major components and transfer them with their shielding to the car. By the time he had finished his shoulders and arms, toughened as they were by regular archery practice, were aching. He drove out through the archway, still without having encountered a soul, and headed south for Hastings.

The drive took rather more than his estimated ninety minutes, and he spent another ten locating the house he had rented at 31 Channing Waye. It turned out to be a reasonably well-preserved 'two-up-and-two-down' in a short row of identical dwellings. The sea was visible at one end of the steeply sloping street. Hutchman felt strangely self-conscious as he put a key into the lock and opened the door of the alien little house he had just acquired. It was legally his, yet he felt guilty of trespass. He walked along the short hall and glanced into the downstairs rooms, noting the sparse furniture which was just sufficient to satisfy the rent-control regulations concerning the letting of houses. The house was cold, lifeless. Filled with an oddly sexual excitement, he went upstairs and found the rear bedroom to be completely empty except for a single bentwood chair painted gooseberry green. The narrow window looked out at a blank wall which ricocheted his thoughts back like bullets.

I may die in this room! The idea leaped into his mind unbidden, bringing with it a depression which countered the shame-tinged arousal the atmosphere of shabby secrecy had inspired in him. He clattered down the stairs and began carrying the machine into the house. The shielding seemed even heavier than before but the distances were short and within ten minutes he had the entire set of components laid out on the floor of the bedroom. He considered beginning the assembly, then decided in favour of an early start back to Crymchurch.

At this stage he had to give priority to letting the world know the machine existed.

'David's asleep, and I'm going out for a couple of hours,' Vicky said from the doorway of his study. She was wearing a rust-coloured tweed suit he could not remember seeing before and her face beneath the carefully applied make-up was taut. A deep sadness gripped Hutchman and he knew that, in spite of everything, he had been hoping she would be satisfied with the blow she had already dealt him.

'Where are you going?'

'I may go and visit Mother.'

'You *may* go and visit your mother.' He laughed drily. 'All right, Vicky – I get the message.'

'That is . . . if you aren't planning to go out,' she said casually, ignoring the implication of his remark. 'I'll stay in and mind David if you're going out.'

Hutchman glanced at the stacks of white paper he had put through the copier. 'No. I'm not going out.'

'That's all right then.' Vicky gave him a speculative look and he guessed she was wondering how he had managed to grow strong. On best form, he should have been on his knees to her, weeping and pleading, grovelling. And he would have done it – that much he had to admit – except that she had made the mistake of overkilling him. One adultery or a dozen, one megaton or a hundred. Hutchman could not plead for his life, because he was already dead.

'I'll see you later,' Vicky said.

Hutchman nodded. 'Give my regards to your mother.'

6

He was relieved, on waking up, to find himself bathed in the special honey-coloured radiance which, he was convinced, the sun emits only on weekend mornings. The effect he surmised to be either objective – fifty million Saturday-conscious Britons influencing the weather by the power of thought – or group-subjective as the same fifty million people created a telepathic blanket of pleasure because the working week was over. In any case, Hutchman was glad he was not required to go into the office because he had to begin mailing those of his envelopes which were destined for the most remote parts of the world. He had decided to split them into small batches and mail them at different post-boxes over as wide an area as he could cover in one day. The area would be confined to the southeast corner of the country, which was less satisfactory than going right up to Scotland, but it would encompass something like a third of the population. And it could be argued that a person living in the north would have deliberately chosen the southeast area to throw investigators off the scent.

Hutchman got out of bed and, in spite of himself, went to the door of the second bedroom and peered in. Vicky was asleep there in the tentlike ambience caused by drawn blinds. He closed the door, went to the bathroom, and washed hastily. There had been no reason to suppose that Vicky would stay out all night but a stubborn and unrealistic part of him felt reassured to find her at home. He dressed in sweater and slacks, and carried all his envelopes out to his car in a suitcase. Before leaving he looked into David's room and stared for a long troubled moment at the small figure in its extravagant posture of sleep.

The mid-morning traffic was relatively light as he drove west, determined to reach Bath before mailing the first envelopes. Any full-scale enquiry into the mailing would start off with a certain amount of ready-made data – the collection times stamped on the envelopes, and the last thing he wanted was to blaze a circular route which started at Crymchurch. He drove quickly, with maximum concentration, and was barely aware of the radio until an hourly newscast mentioned the row which had blown up between the newly formed Damascus Relief Organization and a group of traditional bodies such as Oxfam and UNICEF. A Mr Ryan Rhodes, chairman of DRO, had made a public allegation that postal contributions to his organization had been diverted to other funds with the connivance of the authorities. Hutchman had his doubts about the claim – Rhodes probably was suffering from an attack of charity organizer's cholic – but it occurred to him that, for his own project, he was relying to an inordinate extent on Her Majesty's mails. As a middle-class Englishman he had an inherent faith in institutions like the post office, yet as an intelligent citizen of the late 1980s he understood that no government, not even that of Elizabeth II, obeyed any code of rules.

His forehead pricked coldly. In his case was a sheaf of envelopes addressed to selected Russian statesmen, physicists, and editors of scientific journals – but supposing there was a system in Britain whereby all mail bound for Russia was checked? There were ways to read a letter without opening the envelope. Hutchman eased his foot off the accelerator as he struggled to work out the implications of the new idea. If such a system really were in operation one effect would be that the great manhunt would get under way several days earlier than he had allowed for. This in itself would not necessarily be disastrous, but a much more serious consequence could be that no Russian envelopes would reach their intended destinations. The whole essence of his scheme was that *all* nuclear powers should be informed of the November 10 deadline. If it were used unilaterally Hutchman's antiweapon would automatically become a weapon. Even as it was, by choosing a deadline so close in the future, he had already handicapped the greater powers who would have to work all out to break up their stocks of warheads in time.

As he coasted uncertainly along the road Hutchman was surprised to find the image of a woman's face hovering behind his eyes. It was a smooth, dusky face with a pouting lower lip accented by chalky-pink lipstick. An intelligent amoral face. That of . . . *Andrea Knight!* With the identification came a rush of other information about the woman – she was a biologist with whom Hutchman had been briefly acquainted at university. Lately he had glimpsed her several times in the refectory at the Jeavons Institute, during his rare coffee breaks from work on the machine and – a hard knot of excitement formed in his stomach – he had read something about her in the J.I. Newsletter. She was going to Moscow to take part in a DNA seminar!

Hutchman fought to recall the exact date of her departure, but all he could be certain of was that it was imminent. Perhaps it had already passed, but if she – as a member of an accredited scientific mission – could be persuaded to take an envelope with her there was no doubt that it would get safely through the customs and security barriers. And if he gave her one of the envelopes intended for a journal it should be fairly easy to work out a reasonable story to satisfy her curiosity. If she had already left he would have to think of something else, but it seemed worth his while to find out what the situation was.

The next town ahead was Aldershot. Hutchman accelerated again and within a few minutes was speeding past the neat rows of army housing which spread out for miles on both sides of the road. He stopped at a telephone kiosk near the town and looked up the number of Roger Dufay, the Westfield press officer, who was also a freelance science journalist and a regular contributor to the J.I. Newsletter. The phone rang a longish time but finally was answered by Dufay.

'Hello, Roger!' Hutchman tried to sound hearty and unconcerned. 'Sorry to trouble you at home, but I can't think of anybody else who could answer this one.'

'That's all right, old boy.' Dufay was friendly but cautious. 'What's your problem?'

'I'm trying to contact a friend of mine who's going off to Moscow for the DNA seminar, and I wonder if I'm too late.'

'Mmm. I'm not sure. Who is it you want?'

Hutchman hesitated. He could invent a name but Dufay was one of those frighteningly knowledgeable men who could be capable of reciting the names of the entire British party. 'Ah . . . Andrea Knight.'

'Oho! You're a crafty devil, Hutch. It's like that, is it?'

'No, Roger.' *Not you, too,* Hutchman thought wearily. 'Besides, do you think I'd admit anything to you?'

'No need to, old boy. They don't call our little Andrea the Jeavons bicycle for nothing. You crafty devil.'

'Listen, Roger, have you got a note of when the British party leaves? I'm in a bit of a hurry.'

'I'll bet you are. Hold on a moment.' There was a pause during which Hutchman bent his knees to bring his face level with the kiosk's mirror. His cheeks looked thinner, the line of his jaw standing out clearly, and he had forgotten to shave – for the first time in years. 'Hello, Hutch. They're flying out from Gatwick tomorrow afternoon. So if you want to get in before the commissars you'd better pop round to her place tonight and . . .'

'Thanks, Roger.' Hutchman set the phone down and went in search of the Aldershot general post office. Arriving at it he looked through all the directories covering the Camburn and Crymchurch areas and found the entry he wanted: 'Knight, Andrea, 11 Moore's Road, Camburn . . . Camburn 3436.' He copied it onto a piece of paper and, suddenly apprehensive, dialled the number.

'Andrea Knight here.' She had answered so quickly, even before the phone began to ring properly, that Hutchman was startled.

'Hello, Miss Knight.' He sought the right words. 'I don't know if you would remember me. This is Lucas Hutchman. We were at . . .'

'Lucas Hutchman!' Her voice was surprised, but with undertones of pleasure. 'Of course I remember . . . I've seen you lately at Jeavons, but you didn't speak to me.'

'I wasn't sure if you would know who I was.'

'Well, your not even saying hello to me wouldn't help my memory, would it?'

'I guess not.' Hutchman felt his face grow warm and he realized with mild astonishment that he and this virtual stranger were, within seconds, making contact on a sexual level. 'I always seem to miss my chances.'

'Really? Then why have you rung me? Or shouldn't I be so bold?'

'I was wondering . . .' Hutchman swallowed. 'I know this is very presumptuous, but I was wondering if you would do me a small favour.'

'I hope I can, but I should warn you that I'm leaving

74

for Moscow tomorrow and won't be back for three weeks.'

'It's in connection with your Moscow trip that I'm ringing. I have an article on microwave radiation that I want to get to the editor of *Soviet Science* rather quickly. I could send it through the ordinary mail, but it's quite a fearsome-looking thing – you know how maths papers are – and there's so much censorship and red tape that it might take months before it got through, so I wondered . . .' Hutchman paused to regain his breath.

'Do you want me to deliver it by hand? A sort of trans-Siberian Pony Express?' Andrea laughed easily, and Hutchman felt he had cleared a hurdle.

'No need for anything like that,' he assured her gratefully. 'It'll be in an addressed envelope. If you could simply shove it in a postbox or whatever they have over there.'

'I'll be happy to do that for you, Lucas, but there's a problem.'

'A problem?' Hutchman tried not to sound too concerned.

'Yes. I haven't got the envelope to deliver. How do I get it?'

'That shouldn't be difficult. May I bring it round to you today?'

'Well, I'm still in the throes of packing, but I'll be free this evening if that's convenient.'

Hutchman's heart began to pound steadily. 'Yes, that's fine. Where shall I . . . ?'

'Where do you usually meet women?'

'I . . .' He checked himself from saying that he did not usually meet women. *You asked for this, Vicky.* 'How about the Camburn Arms? Perhaps we could have a meal?'

'I'll look forward to that, Lucas. Eight o'clock?'

'See you at eight o'clock.' He set the phone down and stepped out of the confines of the kiosk into the noonday bustle feeling bewildered, as if he had swallowed several strong gins on an empty stomach. He gazed blankly at the unfamiliar scene for a second before realizing that he was in Aldershot at the beginning of a grand tour of the southern counties. That plan would have to be modified for a start. As he walked back to the car Hutchman decided that posting the first envelopes in a single batch in one town could be less informative to an investigator than an elaborate itinerary. There was something faintly disturbing about the fact that his modified plan for the journey, which had not been considered until a moment ago, seemed better than one he had thought about for days; but there was no denying that it would be wise to ensure a smooth trip for at least one envelope to Moscow.

On the west side of Aldershot he swung south from the Bath road and made the shorter trip to Salisbury where he mailed a sheaf of envelopes. It was not until he was almost back in Crymchurch again that he appreciated the significance of having consigned the antibomb specification to Her Majesty's mails. Until that moment he had retained the option of backing out and returning to sane, normal life.

The first irrevocable step had been taken.

7

Andrea Knight came slowly into the bar, her black hair caught inside the collar of her suede coat, a sling-type handbag almost trailing on the floor. Hutchman, who had arrived a little early, watched as she walked the length of the room. He asked himself what it was about her which caused the male drinkers to fall silent as she passed by. Did the slinky-solvent gait, that chalky and pouting lower lip, suggest something to their minds? The archetypal woman of the streets, composite of Dietrich and Signoret and Hayworth? He gave up the attempted analysis as she reached his table, sat down, and shrugged off her coat without speaking.

'Good to see you.' He spoke quickly. 'Glad you could come.'

'Hello, Lucas. My God, this takes me back more years than I care to remember.'

'I guess it does,' he said, wondering what she was talking about.

'Yes. Did you know the Pack Horse has been demolished to make room for a motorway?'

'No.' Hutchman felt a growing unease.

'Of course, we only had one drink there.' She smiled reproachfully.

Hutchman smiled back at her as the ground seemed to shift below his feet. The Pack Horse was a pub he had used when at university and he had vague memories of having taken girls there – around the time he met Vicky – but surely Andrea had not been one of them. And yet she must have been. It dawned on him that his years with

Vicky had conditioned his very thought processes. (A full year of marital hell-heaven had passed before he had learned always to put his briefcase beside him on the front seat of the car when going home from the office. Vicky, watching like a sniper from the kitchen window, assumed if she saw him remove the case from the rear seat that he had had a passenger. And on the days when he had given a lift but forgot to mention it she spun the delicate but ever tightening webworks of questions, culminating in ghastly midnight confrontations.) He had learned to blot out other women from his memory. A new thought: *Could it be that the monogamous, slightly undersexed person I always imagined myself to be is not the real Lucas Hutchman? Am I a creation of Vicky's? And, in this revenge kick that I'm on, how big a part is played by coincidence and how big a part by subconscious motivation? I saw Andrea at the Jeavons while I was working on the machine. I read about her in the Newsletter and they say the subconscious never forgets details. Details such as the dates of her Moscow trip. Dear Jesus, could it be, could it really be, that the deadline for the operation of my sacred megalife machine was timed to bring me to this table to meet this woman?*

'. . . quite thirsty after the walk,' Andrea was saying. 'My car's in for repairs.'

'Forgive me.' He signalled to the waiter. 'What would you like to drink?'

She asked for a Pernod and sipped it appreciatively. 'A girl with my socialist convictions has no right to order such an expensive drink, but I think I've got a capitalist stomach.'

'That reminds me.' He took the envelope from his inside pocket and handed it to her. 'It's addressed, but you'll need to put a stamp on it for me over there. Do you mind?'

'I don't mind.' She dropped the white rectangle into her handbag without looking at it. Her careless acceptance of the envelope pleased him, but he became worried in case she should be too casual and forget to take it with her.

'It isn't really vital, but it is rather important to me, personally, to have the article delivered soon,' he said.

'Don't worry, Lucas.' She placed her hand on his reassuringly. 'I'll look after it for you.'

Her fingers were cold and he instinctively covered them with his free hand. She smiled again, looking directly into his eyes, and something threw a biological switch in his loins, producing a small distinct thrill as if she had touched him there. Time itself seemed to distort from that moment – individual minutes were fantastically drawn out, but the hours flicked by. They had several drinks, a meal in the adjacent dining room, more drinks, then he drove her to her flat which was the top one in a four-storey building. As soon as the car had crunched to a halt in the gravelled drive she swung out of it and walked to the door, searching in her handbag for a key. At the steps to the door she turned and looked back at him.

'Come on, Lucas,' she said impatiently. 'It's cold out here.'

He got out of the car and went with her into the small lobby. The elevator door was open and they walked into the aluminium box hand in hand. They kissed during the ride up and her mouth was as soft as he had thought it would be, and her thighs – closed around one of his – were as responsive as he had hoped they would be. Hutchman's legs felt slightly shaky as he followed Andrea into her apartment which was pleasantly but sparsely furnished. It smelt faintly of apples. Just inside the door she dropped her coat on her floor and they kissed again. Her body was fuller than Vicky's and her breasts, when he cupped them in his hands, felt heavier than Vicky's.

The automatic and unwanted comparison produced a painful churning sensation behind his eyes. He put Vicky out of his mind and drank from Andrea's mouth.

'Do you want me, Lucas?' Her breath was warm on the roof of his mouth. 'Do you really want me?'

'I really want you.'

'All right then. You wait here.' She walked into a bedroom and he waited without moving till she reappeared. She was wearing nothing but a black peephole brassiere, her nipples angled upward through the apertures on extruded blobs of milky flesh. Breathing noisily, Hutchman removed his own clothes, closed with Andrea, and bore her down onto a flame-coloured rug. *Now*, he thought, *right now, my darling Vicky*.

An indeterminate time went by before he made the shocking discovery that he could feel . . . precisely nothing. It was as if the whole region of his genitals was flooded with a deadening drug, destroying all sensation. Baffled and afraid, he waged a battle between his body and Andrea's, surging and grasping and crushing . . .

'Give it up, Lucas.' Andrea's voice reached him across interstellar distances. 'It isn't your fault.'

'But I don't understand,' he said numbly. 'I don't know what's wrong with me.'

'Sexual hypesthesia,' she replied, not unkindly. 'Krafft-Ebing devotes a whole chapter to it.'

He shook his head. 'But I'm always all right with . . .'

'With your wife?'

'Oh, Christ!' Hutchman pressed his hands to his temples as the pain in his head became intolerable. *What have you done to me, Vicky?*

Andrea stood up, walked to the door where her suede coat was lying, and put it on. 'I've had a very pleasant evening, Lucas, but I have an awful lot to do tomorrow and I must get to bed. Do you mind?'

'Of course not,' he mumbled with senseless formality. As he struggled into his clothes he tried to think of something intelligent and unconcerned to say, and finally came out with, 'I hope you have good flying weather tomorrow.'

Her face betrayed no emotion. 'I hope so too. Good night, Lucas.'

She closed the door quietly. The elevator was still at the landing and he rode down in it, staring at his reflection in the scratched aluminium.

Incredibly, after all that had happened, it was only a little after midnight when he got home, and Vicky was still up. The comfortable old skirt and cardigan she was wearing suggested to him that she had not been out and that no stranger had been in the house during his absence. She was watching the late movie on television and as usual the colour control was turned down too far, producing a faded picture. He adjusted the colour and sat down tiredly without speaking.

'Where have you been this evening, Lucas?'

'Out drinking.'

He waited for her to contradict him, directly or by inference, but she said, 'You shouldn't drink a lot. It doesn't agree with you.'

'It agrees with me better than some things.'

She turned to face him, and spoke hesitantly. 'I get the impression that . . . all this has really hurt you, Lucas, and it surprises me. Did you not understand what you were letting yourself in for?'

Hutchman stared at his wife. He had always loved her most when she wore the sort of friendly, familiar clothes she had on now. Her face was grave and beautiful in the subdued orange light, imbued with the power to make him whole again. He thought of his first batch of envelopes, sorted and separated now, speeding on the first stages of the journeys from which no power of his could bring them back.

'Go to hell, you,' he said thickly and walked out of the room.

Early next morning Hutchman drove east almost as far as Maidstone and dispatched another sheaf of envelopes. The weather was sunny and relatively warm. He got back to the house to find Vicky and David having a late breakfast. The boy was eating cereal and trying to do arithmetic problems at the same time.

'Dad,' he shouted accusingly. 'Why do sums have to have hundreds, tens, and units? Why couldn't it all be units? That way there'd be no carrying to do.'

'It wouldn't work very well, son. But why are you doing homework on a Sunday morning?'

David shrugged. 'The teacher hates me.'

'That's not true, David,' Vicky put in.

'Then why does she give me more sums than the other boys?'

'To *help* you.' Vicky glanced up at Hutchman appealingly. He took David's book and pencil, jotted down the answers to the remaining problems, and handed it back to the boy.

'Thanks, Dad.' David looked at him in wonderment, then darted out of the kitchen whooping with glee.

'Why did you do that?' Vicky lifted the coffeepot, poured an extra cup, and pushed it across the table to Hutchman. 'You've always said that sort of thing didn't help him.'

'We seemed to be immortal in those days.'

'Meaning?'

'Perhaps there isn't enough time to do everything slowly and properly.'

Vicky pressed her hand to her throat. 'I've been watching you, Lucas. You don't act like a man who's been . . .' She sighed. 'What would you say if I told you I hadn't been unfaithful in the clinical sense of the word?'

'I'd say what you've said to me several hundred times in the past – that doing it in the mind is just as bad.'

'But what if it was nauseating to my mind, and I only – '

'What are you trying to do to me?' he demanded harshly, pressing the knuckles of one hand to his lips in case they should tremble. *After all that's happened,* he wondered in panic, *am I going to fall? Can the lady dissolve her homunculus in acid and re-create him at will?*

'Lucas, have you been unfaithful to me?' Her face was that of a priestess.

'No.'

'Then what has all this been about?'

Hutchman, standing with the coffee cup in his hands, felt his knees begin to orbit in minute circles which threatened to become larger and bring him down. A fearsome shift took place in his mind. *Why do I need the machine? The spread of the information is all that matters. World-wide knowledge of how to build the antibomb machine would, by itself, make the possession of any nuclear device too risky. Even if the machine were destroyed my envelopes could still go out as a didactic hoax. Better still, I could open all the remaining envelopes and remove the letter – and just send the information. And without the hardware I could be safe. They need never find me . . .*

He became aware that the telephone was ringing. Vicky half-rose from the table, but he waved her back, hurried impatiently into the hall, and lifted the instrument, cutting it short in the middle of a peal.

'Hutchman speaking.'

'Good morning, Lucas.' The woman's voice seemed to speak to him from another existence, something completely alien and irrelevant to Hutchman as he was on that bright Sunday morning. It took a genuine mental effort for him to identify the speaker as Andrea Knight.

'Hello,' he said uneasily. 'I thought you'd have been at Gatwick by this time.'

'That was the original plan, but I've been transferred to a later flight.'

'Oh!' Hutchman tried to understand why she had rung him. To gloat? To try to make him feel worse by pretending to try to make him feel better?

'Lucas, I'd like to see you today. Can you come round to my flat?'

'Sorry,' he said coldly. 'I don't see any point . . .'

'It's about the envelope you gave me to post for you.'

'Well?' He suddenly found difficulty in breathing.

'I opened it.'

'You *what*?'

'It occurred to me that I should know what I was carrying into Moscow. After all, I'm a practising socialist, and if the article was intended for publication anyway . . .'

'You're a socialist?' he asked faintly.

'Yes. I told you that last night.'

'So you did.' He recalled Andrea saying as much, but then it had seemed unimportant. He took a deep breath. 'Well, what did you think of my little hoax? Childish, isn't it?'

There was a long pause. 'Not very childish, Lucas, no.'

'But I assure you . . .'

'I showed the papers to a friend and he didn't laugh much, either.'

'You'd no right to do that.' He made a feeble attempt at blustering.

'And you'd no right to involve me in something like this. Would you like to come round here and discuss the matter?'

'Just try stopping me.' He threw the phone down and strode into the kitchen. 'Something has come up on the Jack-and-Jill programme. I have to go out for an hour.'

Vicky looked concerned. 'On Sunday? Is it serious?'

'Not serious – just urgent. I'll be back in an hour.'

'All right, Lucas.' She smiled tremulously, in a way that hurt him to see. 'We have to sit down together and talk.'

'I know.' He ran out to his car, broadsided it out onto the road in a turn which sent gravel hissing through the shrubbery like grapeshot, and accelerated fiercely in the direction of Camburn. The traffic was light – with a scattering of people on their way for a pre-lunch drink – and he made good time, the concentration on fast motoring relieving him of the necessity to plan his immediate actions. When he reached the apartment block where Andrea lived it looked unfamiliar in the lemon-coloured sunlight. He stopped the car and glanced up at the top floor. There was nobody at the windows of her flat. He walked quickly to the elevator and rode up in it, staring distastefully at the aluminium walls which in their distorted reflections seemed to store visual records of the previous night's madness. He thumbed Andrea's doorbell, still without taking time to think of what he might say or do. She opened the door within seconds. Her dusky face, with its pouting lower lip, was immobile as she stood aside to let him enter.

'Listen, Andrea,' he said. 'Let's get all the nonsense over with quickly. Give me back my papers and we'll forget the whole thing.'

'I want you to meet Aubrey Welland,' she replied tonelessly.

'Good morning, Mr Hutchman.' A stocky, bespectacled young man, with a square-jawed face and the look of a rugby-playing schoolteacher, emerged from the kitchen. He was wearing a red tie and in the lapel of his tweed jacket was a small, brass hammer-and-sickle badge. He nodded when he saw the direction of Hutchman's gaze. 'Yes, I'm a member of the Party. Have you never seen one before?'

'I didn't come here to play games.' Hutchman was depressingly aware that he sounded like a retired major. 'You have some papers belonging to me, and I want them back.'

Welland appeared to consider the request for a moment. 'Comrade Knight tells me you are a professional mathematician with a special knowledge of nuclear physics.'

Hutchman glanced at Andrea, who eyed him bleakly, and he realized he was getting nowhere by standing on his dignity. 'That's correct. Look, I tried to play a very childish practical joke and now I realize just how stupid it was. Can't we – '

'I'm a mathematician myself,' Welland interrupted. 'Not in your league, of course, but I think I have some appreciation of genuine creative maths.'

'If you had, you'd recognize an outright spoof when you saw one.' An idea formed in the back of Hutchman's mind. 'Didn't you notice the anomaly in the way I handled the Legendre functions?' He smiled condescendingly, and waited.

'No.' Welland lost a little of his composure. He reached into his inside pocket, then changed his mind, and withdrew his hand – but not before Hutchman had glimpsed and identified the corner of a white envelope. 'I'm going to take some convincing about that.'

Hutchman shrugged. 'Let me convince you, then. Where are the papers?'

'I'll keep the papers,' Welland snapped.

'All right.' Hutchman smiled again. 'If you want to make a fool of yourself with your Party bosses, go ahead. To me it's all part of the joke.' He half-turned away, then sprang at Welland, throwing the other man's jacket open with his left hand and grasping the envelope with his right. Welland gasped and clamped his hands over Hutchman's wrists. Hutchman exerted all the power of his bowtoughened muscles, Welland's grip weakened, and the envelope fluttered to the floor. Welland snarled and tried to drag him away from it and they went on a grotesque waltz across the room. The edge of a long coffee table hit the back of Hutchman's legs and to prevent himself going down he stepped up onto it, bringing Welland with him. Welland raised his knee and Hutchman, trying to protect his groin, flung the other man sideways. Too late, he realized they were close to the window. There was an explosive bursting of glass, and suddenly the cool November air was streaming into the room. The lacy material clogged around Hutchman's fingers and mouth as he looked downwards through angular petals of glass. People were running into the forecourt, and a woman was screaming. Hutchman saw why.

Welland had landed on a cast-iron railing and, even from a height of four storeys, it was obvious that he was dead.

8

Detective Inspector Crombie-Carson was a lean, acidulous man who made no concessions to his own or anybody else's humanity. His face was small but crowded with large features, as though all the intervening areas had shrunk and caused the dominant objects to draw together. Horn-rimmed spectacles, a sandy moustache, and one protuberant mole also found room, somehow, on his countenance.

'It's damned unsatisfactory,' he said in clipped military tones, staring with open belligerence at Hutchman. 'You left your home on a Sunday morning and drove from Crymchurch to here to have a drink with Miss Knight?'

'That's it.' Hutchman had been feeling ill since he saw the television-camera team among the crowd below. 'Andrea and I have known each other since our university days.'

'And your wife has no objections to these little excursions?'

'Ah . . . my wife didn't know where I was.' Hutchman drew his lips into the semblance of a smile and tried not to think about Vicky. 'I told her I was going to work for an hour.'

'I see.' Crombie-Carson gazed at Hutchman in disgust. From the start of the interview he had shown no trace of the behind-this-badge-I'm-just-another-human-being attitude with which many police officers eased their relationship with the public. He was doing a job for which he expected to be hated and was more than ready to hate in return. 'How did you feel when you arrived and found that Mr Welland was already here with Miss Knight?'

'I didn't mind – I knew he was here before I set out. I told you I merely stopped by for a drink and a chat.'

'But you told your wife you were going to work.'

'My domestic situation is complicated. My wife is . . . unreasonably jealous.'

'How unfortunate for you.' Crombie-Carson's mouth thinned for an instant, packing his features even closer together. 'It's surprising how many men I encounter who have the same cross to bear.'

Hutchman frowned. 'What are you trying to say, Inspector?'

'I never *try* to say things. I have an excellent command of the language, and my words always convey my exact meaning.'

'You seemed to be implying something more.'

'Really?' Crombie-Carson sounded genuinely puzzled. 'You must have read something into my words, Mr Hutchman. Have you been to this flat on previous occasions?'

'No.' Hutchman made the denial instinctively.

'That's strange. Both the occupants of the ground-floor flat say that your car was . . .'

'During the day, I meant. I was here last night.'

The Inspector permitted himself a little smile. 'Until about 11:30?'

'Until about 11:30,' Hutchman agreed.

'And what excuse did you give your wife last night?'

'I was out drinking.'

'I see.' Crombie-Carson glanced at the uniformed sergeant who was standing beside Andrea, and the sergeant nodded slowly, conveying a message which Hutchman could not understand. 'Now, Miss Knight. As

I understand it, Mr Welland decided to visit you this morning.'

'Yes.' Andrea spoke tiredly, exhaling grey smoke as she stared at the floor.

'Sunday appears to be a busy day for you.'

'On the contrary.' Andrea gave no indication of having seen any semantic shadings in Crombie-Carson's remark. 'I make a point of relaxing on Sundays.'

'Very good. So after Mr Welland had been here for about an hour you decided it would be a good idea for him to meet Mr Hutchman.'

'That's right.'

'Why?'

Andrea raised her eyes. 'Why what?'

'Why did you think a Communist high-school teacher and a guided-missile expert should get together?'

'Their professions or politics didn't come into it. I often introduce my friends to each other.'

'Do you?'

'Of course.' Andrea was pale, but in control of herself. 'Besides, people with dissimilar backgrounds often react together in a more interesting way than . . .'

'I can well believe it.' Crombie-Carson thrust his hands into the pockets of his grey showerproof, walked to the shattered window, and looked down into the street for a moment. 'And this morning, while your two visitors were reacting interestingly with each other, Mr Welland decided to get up on this coffee table and fix your curtains for you?'

'Yes.'

'What was wrong with the curtains?'

'They weren't closing properly. The runners were jamming on the rail.'

'I see.' Crombie-Carson twitched the curtains experimentally. They slid easily along the rail with a series of subdued multiple clicks.

Andrea eyed him squarely. 'Aubrey must have cleared the obstruction before he fell.'

'Probably.' The Inspector nodded morosely. 'If he had still been working on the rail he might have clutched it when he felt the table tip up underneath him. That way he would have pulled panels and everything down – but he mightn't have gone out.'

'I think he had finished,' Hutchman put in. 'I think he was in the act of getting down when the table couped.'

'Couped! An interesting verb, that. Scots, isn't it?'

'I don't know,' Hutchman said warily.

'You were both in the room when the accident happened?'

'Yes, but we weren't looking at the window. There was a crash . . . and he was gone.'

Crombie-Carson gave Andrea a speculative look. 'I understand that as well as teaching mathematics Mr Welland was games master at his school.'

'I believe he was.'

'What an unfortunate time for his reactions to fail him – perhaps he had had too much to drink.'

'No. He hadn't drunk anything.'

The Inspector's face was impassive, compressed. 'Mr Hutchman said he was expecting to have a drink when he got here.'

'I was,' Hutchman replied irritably, 'but not to get stuck into a boozing session the moment I arrived.'

'I see,' Crombie-Carson commented. 'There are certain proprieties to be observed, of course.' He walked slowly around the room, pausing every few paces to make a hissing intake of breath. 'I shall want you both to make written statements. In the meantime, do not make any trips outside the local area without getting permission from me. Come along, sergeant.' The two policemen left the apartment with a final look around, and during the moment the door was open men's voices flooded in from the landing, raucous and eager.

'Pleasant fellow,' Hutchman said. 'Ex-colonial police, I'd say.'

Andrea jumped up from the couch and advanced on him, head thrust forward. 'I should have told the truth. I should have handed you over.'

'No, you did the right thing. Communize the cloisters as much as you want to, but don't get any deeper into this business. Believe me, Andrea, all hell is going to break loose very shortly.'

'Shortly?' Andrea snorted.

'That's right. I assure you – you've seen nothing yet.' *I sounded like Leslie Howard as Pimpernel Smith,* Hutchman thought, as he let himself out. Several waiting men flashed press cards in his face, crowded around, and followed him into the elevator. Their presence helped him to sustain the role. He forced himself to sound civilized and unperturbed as he repeated the story of the accident, but when he got into the car his legs began to tremble so violently that he was almost unable to operate the foot pedals. The car jerked away from the knot of people gathered outside the building and as he turned it towards Crymchurch he noticed with a dull sense of shock that the sky was darkening. He had left home in mid-morning, telling Vicky he was going to the office for one hour – and she had believed him. Just as they had reached the far side of despair she had, for some reason lost in the complexities of the human condition, begun to believe in him. Now he was returning to her with the dusk, bringing as much pain as any two people could bear. Hutchman touched the white envelope in his pocket. Supposing he showed its contents to Vicky? At least one other person, still alive, had seen his work, so why not Vicky? Would it convince her? Would it make any difference to anything? Could he justify involving her to that extent just as the human chain reaction triggered off by his actions was on the point of becoming super-critical? The explosion was coming, inevitably, and he was going to be at the centre of it. He was ground zero.

The house, with its warm lights glowing through the screen of poplars, looked achingly peaceful. He parked his car and stood outside for a moment, reluctant to enter, then went in through the side door. The interior, although brightly lit, was very quiet – and empty. He walked through to the lounge and found a note in Vicky's handwriting sitting on the stone fireplace. It said: 'The police have been here. Several reporters have rung me. And I have heard the news on the radio. I was beginning to hope I was wrong about you. I have taken David. This time – and I *am* sane – it is finally over. V. H.' Hutchman said aloud, 'You, too, have done the right thing.'

He sat down and, with meaningless deliberation, looked around the room. Nothing in it, he discovered, was of any importance. The walls, the pictures, and the furniture had become slightly unreal. They were stage properties among which three people had, for a while, acted out assigned roles. Suddenly conscious that he was artificially extending his own part beyond its term, he got to his feet and went into his study. There were more than a hundred envelopes – including those destined for England – yet to be filled, sealed, addressed, and stamped. He threw himself into the mechanical tasks, concentrating on minute details of folding the papers and exactly squaring the stamps to further deaden the ponderous workings of his mind. The attempt was moderately successful, but at times strange, incredible thoughts came to the fore.

My wife and child have left me.

Today I killed a man. I lied about it to the police and

they let me go, but I knew that I did it. I didn't mean to do it, but it happened. I terminated a human life!

The news about my machine is spreading across the world. Soon the information ripple is going to reach the confines of its system, and then the direction will be reversed. I'm at the centre. I'm the ground zero man, and terrible things are going to happen to me.

My wife and child have left me . . .

When the work was finished and the envelopes piled in neat stacks, Hutchman looked around blankly, faced with the prospect of going on living. It occurred to him that he had not eaten anything all day, but the thought of preparing food was preposterous. The only meaningful action he could think of was to take another batch of envelopes out and mail them, possibly in London. Just at the time he most needed to preserve his obscurity he had been catapulted into the news headlines, yet it was still worthwhile to cover his tracks as regards the mailings. The police knew he had been involved in a peculiar accident – they still had nothing to make him a suspect in the massive security investigation which would ensue when the first envelope reached Whitehall. Andrea had half-threatened to tell the police all she knew, but what she really wanted was to disengage herself as rapidly and completely as possible. There was no danger there.

Hutchman brought the small suitcase in from the car and refilled it with envelopes. He turned off all the lights, went out into the blustery, rain-seeded darkness, and locked the door. *Force of habit,* he thought. *What is there to steal?* He threw the case onto the front seat of the car and was in the act of getting in beside it when a brilliant beam of light slewed across the drive, making shadows leap. A black sedan materialized behind the lights and crunched to a halt close to his car. Three men got out immediately, but Hutchman could not see them clearly because a spotlight was shining into his eyes. He fought to contain his fear.

'Going somewhere, Mr Hutchman?' The voice was hard and disapproving, but Hutchman relaxed as he identified it as belong to Detective Inspector Crombie-Carson.

'No,' he said easily. 'Just doing a local errand.'

'With a suitcase?'

'With a suitcase. They're handy for carrying things around. What can I do for you, Inspector?'

Crombie-Carson approached the car, the police spotlight pinpointing him with radiance. 'You can answer some more questions.'

'But I've told you all I know about Welland.'

'That remains to be seen,' the Inspector snapped. 'However, it's Miss Knight I'm interested in now.'

'Andrea!' Hutchman felt a sick premonition. 'What about her?'

'Earlier this evening,' Crombie-Carson said coldly, 'she was abducted from her apartment by three armed men.'

9

'Good God,' Hutchman whispered. 'Why should anybody want to do that?'

Crombie-Carson gave a short laugh which somehow indicated that, while he appreciated Hutchman's display of surprise on its merits purely as a display, he had seen many guilty men react in a similar manner. 'A lot of people would like to know the answer to that question. Where, for instance, have you been all evening?'

'Right here. At home.'

'Anybody with you to substantiate that?'

'No.' *If Andrea has been abducted*, Hutchman thought belatedly, *then she must have talked to more people than Welland. Either that or Welland passed something on to . . .*

'How about your wife?'

'No. Not my wife – she's staying with her parents.'

'I see,' Crombie-Carson said, using what Hutchman was beginning to recognize as an all-purpose phrase. 'Mr Hutchman, I suspect that you were about to leave this area in spite of my request that you should remain.'

Hutchman felt stirrings of real alarm. 'I assure you I wasn't. Where would I go?'

'What have you in that suitcase?'

'Nothing.' Hutchman squinted into the spotlight, feeling mild heat from it on his face. 'Nothing like what you're looking for. It's correspondence.'

'Do you mind showing it to me?'

'I don't mind.' Hutchman opened the car door, pulled the case to the edge of the seat, and clicked it open. The light played on the bundles of envelopes and reflected in the Inspector's glasses.

'Thank you, Mr Hutchman – I had to be certain. Now if you would lock the case away in your car or in the house, I would like you to accompany me to Crymchurch police station.'

'Why should I?' The situation, Hutchman realized, had gone far beyond his control.

'I have reason to believe you can help me with my inquiries.'

'Is that another way of saying I'm under arrest?'

'No, Mr Hutchman. I have no reason to arrest you, but I can require you to give your full co-operation during my investigations. If necessary I can . . .'

'Don't bother,' Hutchman said, feigning resignation. 'I'll go with you.' He closed the case, put it on the floor of the car, and locked the door. Crombie-Carson ushered him into the rear seat of the police cruiser and got in beside him. The interior smelt of wax polish and dusty air circulated by the heater. Hutchman sat upright, acutely self-conscious, watching the flowing patterns of lights beyond the windows with heightened awareness, like a child going on holiday or a man being wheeled into an operating theatre. He was unaccustomed to riding in a back seat, and the car felt monstrously long, unwieldy. The uniformed driver seemed to manoeuvre it around corners with super-human skill. It was almost ten o'clock by the time they got into the town and the public houses were busy with the Sunday night trade. Hutchman glimpsed the yellow-lit windows of Joe's inn and abruptly his sense of adventure deserted him. He longed to be going into Joe's for the last congenial hour, not for spirits but for pints of creamy stout which he could swill and swallow and drown in until it was time to go home. As the car swung into the police station Hutchman, who normally never drank stout or beer, felt that he had to have at least one pint, perhaps as a token that he could still contact the normal, mundane world.

'How long is this going to take?' he said anxiously to Crombie-Carson, speaking for the first time since he had got into the car.

'Oh, not very long. It's quite a routine matter, really.'

Hutchman nodded. The Inspector had sounded quite affable, and he privately estimated that he could be out again in thirty minutes, giving him at least another thirty for a beer, a chat with friends he had never met before, and a peek down the landlady's blouse . . . A man with no family ties could take his fill of such simple pleasures. The last was a meagre compensation, almost inconsiderable, but memories of his abysmal failure with Andrea – perhaps Vicky's hold would relax now that she had renounced all rights. And Andrea had come on too strong that night. Was it only *last* night? *Where is she now? And what is Vicky doing? Where is David? What's happening to me?* He blinked at his surroundings in internally generated alarm.

'This way, Mr Hutchman.' Crombie-Carson led him through a side entrance from the vehicle park, along a corridor, past an area containing an hotel-like reception desk and potted palms, and into a small sparsely furnished room. 'Please sit down.'

'Thank you.' Hutchman got a gloomy feeling it would take him more than thirty minutes to extricate himself.

'Now.' Crombie-Carson sat down at the other side of a metal table without removing his showerproof. 'I'm going to ask you some questions and the constable here is going to make a shorthand note of the interview.'

'All right,' Hutchman said helplessly, wondering how much the Inspector knew or suspected.

'Good. I take it that, as a condition of your employment, you are familiar with the provisions of the Official Secrets Act and have signed a document binding you to observe the Act?'

'I have.' Hutchman thought back to the meaningless scrap of paper he had signed on joining Westfield's and which had never influenced his activities in any way.

'Have you ever revealed any details of your work for Westfield's to a third party who was not similarly bound by the Act?'

'No.' Hutchman began to relax slightly. Crombie-Carson was barking up the wrong tree and could continue to do so for as long as he wanted.

'Did you know that Miss Knight is a member of the Communist Party?'

'I didn't know she actually carried a card, but I'd an idea she had socialist leanings.'

'You knew that much, did you?' The Inspector's condensed face was alert.

'There's no harm in that, is there? Some of the shop stewards in our missile-production factory are red-hot Party men who go to Moscow for their holidays. It doesn't mean they're secret agents.'

'I'm not concerned with your trade-union officials, Mr Hutchman. Have you ever discussed your work at Westfield's with Miss Knight?'

'Of course not. Until yesterday I hadn't even spoken to her for years. I . . .' Hutchman regretted the words as soon as they were uttered.

'I see. And why did you re-establish contact?'

'No special reason.' Hutchman shrugged. 'I saw her accidentally at the Jeavons Institute the other day and yesterday I rang her. For old times' sake, you might say.'

'*You* might. What did your wife say?'

'Listen, Inspector.' Hutchman gripped the cool metal

of the table. 'Do you suspect me of betraying my country or my wife? You've got to make up your mind which.'

'Really? I wasn't aware that the two activities were in any way incompatible. In my experience they often go hand in hand. Surely the Freudian aspect of the typical spy fantasy is one of its most dominant features.'

'That's as may be.' Hutchman was shaken by the relevance of the Inspector's comment – there had been that terrible moment of self-doubt, of identity blurring, just after he had met Andrea in the Camburn Arms. 'However, I have not committed adultery or espionage.'

'Is your work classified?'

'Moderately. It is also very boring. One of the reasons I'm so positive I've never discussed it with anybody is that nothing would turn them off quicker.'

Crombie-Carson stood up, removed his coat, and set it on a chair. 'What do you know about Miss Knight's disappearance?'

'Just what you told me. Have you no clue about where she is?'

'Have you any idea why three armed men should go to her apartment, forcibly drag her out of it, and take her away?'

'None.'

'Have you any idea who did it?'

'No. Have you?'

'Mr Hutchman,' the Inspector said impatiently, 'let's conduct this interview the old-fashioned way. It's always more productive when I ask the questions.'

'All right – but permit me to be concerned about the welfare of a friend. All you tell me is . . .'

'A friend? Would acquaintance not be a better word?'

Hutchman closed his eyes. 'Your use of the language is very precise.'

At that moment the door opened and a sergeant came

into the room with a buff folder. He set it on the table in front of Crombie-Carson and left without speaking. The Inspector glanced through it and took out eight photographs. They were not typical police-record pictures, but whole-plate shots of men's faces, some of them portraits and others apparently blown up from sections of crowd photographs. Crombie-Carson spread them in front of Hutchman.

'Study these faces closely, and tell me if you've seen any of them before.'

'I don't remember ever seeing any of these men,' Hutchman said after he had scanned the pictures. He lifted the edge of one and tried to turn it over, but Crombie-Carson's hand pressed it down again.

'I'll take those.' The Inspector gathered up the glossy rectangles and returned them to the folder.

'If you have finished with me,' Hutchman said carefully, 'I have a craving for a pint of stout.'

Crombie-Carson laughed incredulously and glanced at the shorthand writer with raised eyebrows. 'You haven't a hope in hell.'

'But what more do you want from me?'

'I'll tell you. We have just completed part one of the interview. Part one is the section in which I treat the interviewee gently and with the respect a ratepayer deserves – until it becomes obvious he is not going to co-operate. That part is over now, and you've made it clear you are not going to be helpful of your own accord. From now on, Mr Hutchman, I am going to lean on you. More than a little.'

Hutchman gaped at him. 'You can't! You have nothing against me.'

Crombie-Carson leaned across the table. 'Give me some credit, friend. I'm a professional. Every day in life I'm up against other professionals and I nearly always win. Did you seriously think I would let a big soft amateur like you stand in my way?'

'An amateur at what?' Hutchman demanded, concealing his panic.

'I don't know exactly what you've been up to – *yet* – but you've done something. You're also a very poor liar, but I don't mind that because it makes things easier for me. What I really object to about you is that you're a kind of walking disaster area.'

I'm the ground zero man, a voice chanted in Hutchman's head. 'What do you mean?'

'Since you quietly slipped out of your fashionable bungalow this morning one woman has been abducted and two men have died.'

'*Two* men! I don't . . .'

'Did I forget to tell you?' Crombie-Carson was elaborately apologetic. 'One of the three men who abducted Miss Knight shot and killed a passer-by who tried to interfere.'

Part two of the interview was every bit as bad as Hutchman had been led to expect. Seemingly endless series of questions, often about trivia, shouted or whispered, throwing coils of words around his mind. Implications which if not immediately spotted and challenged hedged him in, drove him closer and closer to telling the wrong lie or the wrong truth. *Grazing ellipsis,* Hutchman thought at one stage, his exhaustion creating a feeling – akin to the spurious cosmic revelation of semiwakefulness – that he had produced the greatest pun of all time. So numbed was he by the end of the ordeal that he was in bed in a neat but windowless 'guest room' on an upper floor of the station before realizing he had not been given the option of going home to sleep. He stared resentfully at the closed door for a full minute, telling himself he would kick up hell if it proved to be locked. But he had had virtually no sleep for forty-eight hours, his brain had been savaged by Crombie-Carson, and although he was going to stand no nonsense about the door, it seemed hardly worth while doing anything about it before morning . . .

He dropped cleanly into sleep.

The sound of the door being opened wakened him. Convinced he had been asleep only a few minutes, Hutchman glanced at his watch and found that it registered ten past six. He sat up, becoming aware that he was wearing grey linen pyjamas, and watched the doorway as a young uniformed constable came in carrying a cloth-covered tray. The small room filled with the smell of bacon and strong tea.

'Good morning, sir,' the constable said. 'Here's your breakfast. I hope you like your tea nearly solid.'

'I don't mind.' Hutchman's preference was for weak tea, but his thoughts were occupied by something infinitely more important. This was Monday – and the remainder of his envelopes should have been in the mail. A crushing sense of urgency dulled his voice. 'I take it I'm free to leave here at any time?'

The fresh-faced constable removed the tray cloth and folded it meticulously. 'That's something you would need to raise with Inspector Crombie-Carson, sir.'

'You mean I'm *not* free to leave?'

'That's a matter for the Inspector.'

'Don't give me that. You fellows on duty at the desk must receive instructions about who is allowed to leave and who isn't.'

'I'll tell the Inspector you want to see him.' The constable set the tray across Hutchman's thighs and walked to the door. 'Don't let your scrambled egg get cold – there's only one sitting for breakfast.'

'Just a minute! Is the Inspector here now?'

'No, sir. He had a long day and has gone home to sleep. He'll probably be here in the afternoon.'

The door closed on the constable's final word before Hutchman could put the tray aside, and he realized it had been set on his knees deliberately to immobilize him. He slid it onto the bedside locker and went to the door. It was locked. He walked around the featureless perimeter of the room, arrived back at the bed, and sat down. The strips of bacon looked underdone, the fat still translucent, and too much butter had been used in the scrambled eggs, making them a greasy yellow mush. Hutchman lifted the mug of tea and sipped it experimentally. It was over-sweet and much too strong, but hot. He held the mug in both hands and slowly drank the brown brew, deriving satisfaction from the tiny thrill which coursed through the nerves in his temples at every sip. The tea had no food value but at least it helped him to think.

Monday afternoon would probably be time enough to post the last of the envelopes, but what guarantee was there that he would be out by then? The constable had said Crombie-Carson would *probably* be at the station in the afternoon, and even if he did show up nobody was obliged to report his presence to Hutchman. And, going one step further, the Inspector could at that stage put his cards on the table and say he intended to hold onto Hutchman for several days or longer. Hutchman vainly tried to recall his own legal rights. He knew that the powers of the police, including that of detaining without showing cause, had been extended recently as part of the Establishment's tougher measures to combat epidemic violence. In the security of his previous existence he had approved of the police having more authority, on the rare occasions when the idea crossed his mind, but now it seemed intolerable.

The galling thing was that he knew why he should have been held, and had no idea of why the police thought they were holding him. Welland was dead, Andrea had been snatched from her apartment, and an innocent third party had been murdered on the street. All these things – as Crombie-Carson's intuition so rightly told him – were a direct result of Hutchman's activities. And what was happening to Andrea at this minute? If the Russians – or anybody else, for that matter – had got hold of her she would soon tell all she knew. Once that happened they could communicate with Whitehall, because Hutchman had put himself beyond mere international rivalries, and a detachment of faceless men would come to Crymchurch for him.

Hutchman finished the tea, grimacing as the undissolved sugar silted into his mouth. By building the machine he had declared open season on himself. No matter who disposed of him there would be drinks in brown rooms in Whitehall, in Peking and Paris. And all he was doing was sitting quietly in Government-issue pyjamas, like a trembling moth waiting to be dropped into the killing bottle. They could come at any minute. At any second!

With a convulsive excess of energy, he leapt to his feet and looked for his clothes. His slacks, sweater, and brown-suede jacket were hanging in a built-in closet. He dressed quickly and checked through his pockets. All his belongings were intact, including a roll of money – remainder of what Vicky had given him to deposit in the bank – and a tiny penknife. The blade of the latter was about an inch long, making it a less effective weapon than fist or foot. He looked helplessly around the room, then went to the door and began kicking it with the flat of his foot, slowly and rhythmically, striving for maximum impact. The door absorbed the shocks with disappointingly little sound, but he had been doing it for only a few minutes when he heard the lock clicking. When the door opened he saw the same young constable and a thin-lipped sergeant.

'What's the game?' the sergeant demanded indignantly. 'Why were you kicking the door?'

'I want out of here.' Hutchman began walking, trying to breast the sergeant out of his way. 'You've no right to keep me locked up.'

The sergeant pushed him back. 'You're staying until the Inspector says you can go. And if you start kicking the door again I'll cuff your hands to your ankles. Got it?'

Hutchman nodded meekly, turned away, then darted through the doorway. Miraculously, he made it out into the corridor and ran straight into the arms of a third policeman. This man seemed larger than the other two put together, a tidal wave of blue uniform which swept Hutchman up effortlessly on its crest and hurled him back into the room.

'That was stupid,' the sergeant remarked. 'Now you're in for assaulting an officer. If I felt like it, I could transfer you to a cell – so make the best of things in here.'

He slammed the door, leaving Hutchman more alone and more of a prisoner than he had been previously. His upper lip was throbbing where it had come in contact with a uniform button. He paced up and down the room, trembling, trying to come to terms with the fact that he really was a prisoner and – no matter how righteous his cause, no matter how many human lives depended on him – the walls were not going to be riven by a thunderbolt. *This is crazy*, he thought bleakly. *I can make neutrons dance – can I not outwit a handful of local bobbies?* He sat down on the room's only chair and made a conscious effort to think his way to freedom. Presently he walked across to the bed and pulled the sheets away from it, exposing a thick foam-plastic mattress.

He stared at it for a moment, then took out his penknife and began cutting the spongy material. The tough outer skin resisted his efforts at first but the cellular interior parted easily. Fifteen minutes later he had cut a six-foot-long, coffin-shaped piece out of the centre of the mattress. He rolled the piece up, compressed it as much as possible and crammed it into the bedside locker, closing the door on it with difficulty. That done, he got into the bed and lay on the area of spring exposed by his surgery on the mattress. It depressed a little with his weight, but the plastic mattress remained on approximately its original level, an inch or so higher than his face. Satisfied with his achievement, he sat upright and pulled the sheets up over the mattress again. Working from underneath, it was an awkward task to get the pillows and bedding disposed in such a way as to resemble normal untidiness, and he was sweating by the time he had finished.

He lay perfectly still, and waited, suddenly aware that he was still very short on sleep . . .

Hutchman was awakened from an involuntary doze by the sound of the door opening. He held his breath to avoid even the slightest disturbance of the sheet just above his face. A man's voice swore fervently. There was a rush of heavy footsteps to the bed, into the screened-off toilet facility in the corner, to the closet, and back to the bed again. The unseen man grunted almost in Hutchman's ear as he knelt to look under the bed. Hutchman froze with anxiety in case the downward bulge of the spring would give him away, but the footsteps retreated again.

'Sergeant,' a dwindling voice called in the corridor, 'he's gone!'

The door appeared to have been left open, but Hutchman resisted the temptation to make a break. His scanty knowledge of police psychology was vindicated a few seconds later when other footsteps, a small party of men this time, sounded in the corridor, running. They exploded into the room, carried out the same search pattern as before, and retreated into the distance. Hutchman's straining ears told him the door of the room had not been closed. His plan had achieved optimum success so far, but had reached a stage at which some delicate judgment was required. Would the police assume he had escaped from the premises, or would a search of the building be instigated? If the latter, he would be better to remain where he was for a while – yet there was a definite risk in remaining too long. Someone had only to come in to make up the bed . . .

He waited for what felt like twenty minutes, growing more nervous, listening to the sounds of a building in use – doors slamming, distant telephones ringing, occasional blurred shouts or laughs. Twice he heard footsteps moving unconcernedly along outside the room and once they were those of a woman, but he was lucky in that the corridor appeared not too frequented at that time of the day. At last he was satisfied that the building was not being systematically combed. He threw off the sheet and climbed out of the bed. Stepping out into the corridor seemed a hideous risk, but he gathered all the bedding up into a great ball and carried it out of the room. The group of men who had searched for him had come from the right, so Hutchman turned left. He moved along the corridor, scanning doors from behind his carapace of white linen. At the very end he found a grey-painted metal door with 'FIRE EXIT' stencilled on it in red. He opened the door and, still carrying the bedding, went down the narrow stairs of bare concrete. At the bottom he pushed open a heavy door and found himself looking out at the steely light of mid-morning streaming across a small car park. There were few cars in it, and no people.

Hutchman walked boldly across the park and through an open gateway into Crymchurch High Street. The police station was on his left. He turned away from it and went along the street, restraining himself from breaking into a run, his face buried in the flapping linen. At the first corner he turned right, only then permitting himself the luxury of feeling he had got clear. The sense of partial relaxation did not last long.

I'm miles away from home, he thought. *And that's where the envelopes are.*

He considered looking for a taxi, then remembered they were a rarity in Crymchurch. The idea of stealing a car was somehow more shocking, on its own level, than anything else he had done since he had broken all ties with society. It would be his first outright criminal act – and he was not even certain he could do it – but there was no good alternative. He began examining the dashboards of the cars parked along the street on which he was walking. Two blocks further along, where Crymchurch's business section was shading into a residential area, he spotted the gleam of keys in an ignition switch. The car was not the best sort for his purpose – it was one of the new Government-subsidized safety models, with four high-backed aft-facing seats and only the driver's seat facing forward. All such cars had a governor on the engine which limited the top speed to a hundred kilometers per hour.

On consideration, Hutchman decided he would be better not to break any speed regulations anyway. He glanced around to make sure the owner was not in sight, dropped the bedding on the footpath, and got into the car. It started at the first turn of the key, and he drove away smoothly but quickly. *Not bad for a big soft amateur,* he thought in a momentary childish glee. *But beware of hubris, Hutch, old son!*

He circled the outskirts of the town, gradually adjusting to the feel of the unfamiliar controls, and once was shocked when he glimpsed his unshaven face in the driving mirror. It was a tired and desperate face, one which belonged to a hunted stranger. On reaching his house he drove slowly past it, satisfying himself that there were no police around, then halted and backed into the driveway. His own car, windows opaqued with moisture, was sitting where he had left it. He parked the stolen car close to the shrubbery and got out, staring nostalgically at the house and wondering what he would do if he saw Vicky at a window. But the two milk bottles still sitting on the doorstep told him she had not returned. Symbols. Two quotation marks which signified the end of the dialogue with Vicky. His eyes blurred painfully.

He searched in his pockets, found the ignition key of his own car. It, too, started at the first turn of the switch and a minute later he was driving northward, towards winter.

10

The whole broad back of the country lay before him, daunting in its size, complexity, and possibilities of danger. He had been accustomed to thinking of Britain as a cosy little island, a crowded patch of grass which scarcely afforded a jetliner space to trim for level flight before it was time for it to nestle down again. Now, suddenly, the land was huge and misty, crawling with menace, magnified in inverse proportion to the number of human beings to whom he could turn for help.

Hutchman drove steadily, aware of the consequences of a speeding offence or even the slightest accident. He watched the mirror more than usual, cursing the other cars which hung near his offside rear wheel, bristling with kinetic energy, always about to overtake yet paradoxically frozen in formation with him. Other drivers, secure and separated in their own little Einsteinian systems of relative movement, met his eyes with mild curiosity until he put on his Polaroids, investing the windscreen with a pattern of oily blue squares. He crossed the Thames at Henley and drove northwest in the direction of Oxford, stopping at isolated mailboxes to post small bundles of his envelopes.

By midday Hutchman was deep in the Tolkien-land of the Cotswolds, swishing through villages of honey-coloured stone which seemed to have grown by some natural process rather than artifice. Domesticated valleys shone in pale tints beneath veils of white mist. He surveyed the countryside in detached gloom, his brain seething with regrets and reconsiderations, until the mention of his name on a newscast brought him back to the minute-by-minute business of living. The car radio crackled as he turned up the volume, causing him to lose part of the item.

'. . . *intensive police activity centred on the house in Moore's Road, Camburn, where two men died yesterday, one of them as a result of a fall from an upper window, the other shot dead when the biology lecturer Andrea Knight was abducted from her apartment by three armed men. The man who fell to his death was Mr Aubrey Welland, a schoolteacher, of 209 Ridge Road, Upton Green; and the man who was shot during the gangster-style abduction was fifty-nine-years-old Mr Richard Thomas Bilson, of 38 Moore's Road, Camburn, who was passing by at the time and is understood to have tried to prevent the three men from pushing Miss Knight into a car. The police have no known clues as to the present whereabouts of Miss Knight, but both she and Welland were members of the Communist Party, and it is thought that her disappearance may have some political motivation.*

'*Latest development in the case is that thirty-nine-years-old Mr Lucas Hutchman, of Priory Hill, Crymchurch, a mathematician with the guided-weapons firm of Westfield's, is being sought by the police, who believe he can materially assist with their inquiries. Hutchman was taken to Crymchurch police station last night, but disappeared this morning. He is described as six-feet tall, black-haired, slim-built, clean-shaven, wearing grey slacks and a brown-suede jacket. He is thought to be driving a pale-blue Ford Sierra, registration number B836 SMN. Anybody seeing this car or a man answering to Hutchman's description should contact their nearest police station immediately . . .*

'*Reports of a serious fire on board the orbiting laboratory have been denied by . . .*'

Hutchman turned the radio down until it was producing background noise. His first thought was that somebody had been *fast*. Scarcely three hours had elapsed since he had walked out of Crymchurch police station, which indicated that the police had not waited for reporters to uncover the facts but had gone to the BBC and enlisted their air. He did not know much about police procedures, but memory told him that outright appeals on the public broadcasting system were fairly rare events. The signs were that Crombie-Carson, or somebody above him, had an idea that something really big was talking place. Hutchman glanced in his mirror. There was a car a short distance behind, belatedly rising and sinking on the irregularities of the hedge-lined road. Was that silvery flash an aerial? Had the driver been listening to the same newscast? Would he recall the description of the car if he overtook? Hutchman depressed the accelerator instinctively and pulled ahead until the following vehicle was lost from view, but then found himself drawing closer to another car. He fell back a little and tried to think constructively.

The main reason he needed transport of his own was so that he could diffuse his mailings over a wide area, and do it quickly. All the envelopes had to be in the mails before the last collection of the day. Once that was done he could abandon the car – except that it might be found almost immediately, giving the police an accurate pointer to his location. His best solution seemed to be to examine the main points of the broadcast description and decide which of them really were invariants . . .

Reaching the outskirts of Cheltenham he parked the car in a quiet avenue and, leaving his jacket in it, took a bus into the centre of the town. Sitting on the upper deck he took the roll of notes from his pocket and counted it. The total was £338, which was more than enough to take

113

care of his needs until D-Day. On descending from the
bus in the unfamiliar shopping centre he found himself
shivering in the sharp November air, and decided that
walking about in slacks and a worsted sweater could
make him too conspicuous. He went into an outfitter's
and bought a zippered grey jacket. In a nearby general
store he acquired a battery-powered electric razor and
while trying it out trimmed his stubble into the beginnings
of a signoral beard. It was only three days old, but the
blackness and thickness of the growth made it acceptable
as a beard which would register as part of his appearance.

Feeling more secure, Hutchman found an auto-
accessory shop which supplied reflective number plates
on a while-you-wait basis. He composed an unremarkable
licence number, ordered two new plates bearing it, and –
after a five-minute delay during which the digits were
bonded to the base – emerged in chilly sunlight with his
purchase under his arm.

A sharp pang of hunger startled him, then he remembered that his last food had been taken with Andrea,
back in another existence. The thought of a hot meal in a
restaurant was tempting but he could not spare the time.
He bought a plastic shopping bag and partially filled it
with six aerosol cans of black automobile paint and a
bottle of thinners. These he obtained in small lots in
three different shops to avoid giving any perceptive sales
assistant the idea that he was going to paint a complete
car. Topping the bag up with cellophane-wrapped sandwiches and cans of stout – the odd craving of the previous
night had not entirely left him – he caught a bus back out
of town along the same road.

Disembarking from the bus he approached his car
warily. The whole expedition had taken little more than
an hour, but there had been plenty of time for the car to
have been observed and reported. When satisfied there

114

was no unusual activity in the area he got into the driving seat and drove eastward into the hills, looking for a quiet spot in which he could work without attracting any attention. Nearly thirty minutes had passed before he found a suitably secluded lane. It led towards a disused farm building and was well screened with hawthorns. He parked out of sight of the main road and at once went to work with the aerosols, spraying the paint on in great cloudy swathes. To do the job properly he should have masked the glass and chrome before starting, but he contented himself by cleaning them with a handkerchief soaked in thinners each time a wisp of paint went astray. By spraying thinly and not being too particular about details he transformed his pale blue car into a black car in less than twenty minutes. He threw the empty aerosols into the ditch, took a screwdriver from the car's tool kit and changed the number plates, throwing the old plates into the boot.

As soon as the job was finished his hunger returned in full strength. He ate his sandwiches quickly, washing them down with mouthfuls of Guinness, and reversed the car up to the road. Resisting the urge to travel faster to make up for lost time, he drove at a conservative speed, never exceeding a hundred kilometers an hour. Villages and towns ghosted past, and by dusk the character of the countryside was changing. The buildings were of darker stone and the vegetation of a deeper green, mistfed, nourished by the soot-ridden atmosphere which had once existed in the industrial north and had left its legacy of enriched soil.

Hutchman began stopping briefly in large towns and mailing bunches of envelopes at central post offices to cut out one stage of the collection process. He reached Stockport early in the evening, posted the last envelopes – and discovered that the itinerant mission, with its series of short-term goals, had been the only thing that was holding him together. There was nothing for him to do now but wait until it was time to return south to Hastings for his rendezvous with the megalives machine. With the hiatus in the demand for physical activity came a rush of sadness and self-pity. The weather was still cold and dry, so he walked down to the blackly flowing Mersey and tried to arrange his thoughts. Emotional tensions were building up inside him, the sort of tensions which he had always understood could be relieved by crying the way a woman does when a situation becomes too much for her.

Why not do it, then? The thought was strange and repugnant, but he was on his own now, relieved from society's constraints, and if weeping like a child would ease the strangling torment in his thorax . . . He sat down guiltily on a wood-slatted seat on the edge of a small green, rested his head on his hands, and tried to cry.

Vicky, he thought, and his mouth slowly dragged itself out of shape. Unrelated image-shards swirled in his mind as his nostalgia for the life he had discarded became unbearable: Vicky's smile of pleasure as he agreed to make love her way and let her bestride him; the smell of pine needles and mince pies at Christmas; the coolness of a freshly laundered shirt; walking into the toilet immediately after David and finding it not flushed, with his son's small stools (studded with the chewing gum he insisted on swallowing) floating in the bowl; going shopping for trivia with Vicky on a summer morning and the both of them getting tipsy before lunch without having bought any of the items they went out to get; glowing pictures in the gloom – a line from Sassoon, but relevant enough to be appropriate – and friendly books that hold me late; looking out at his archery butt on a morning when the dew had dulled the grass, making it visually inert, as though seen through polarized glass . . .

But his mouth remained frozen in the original contortion. His pain grew more intense, yet the tears refused to come.

Finally, swearing bitterly and feeling cheated, Hutchman got to his feet and walked back to his car through black streets which were battlegrounds for tides of cold air. The familiar smell and feel of the car was momentarily comforting. He filled the tank at a self-service station and made a conscious effort to be more constructive in his thinking – the episode by the river had been distressing and futile. The last of the envelopes, including those bound for destinations in Britain, had been mailed and tomorrow they would be read by people in high places. There could be a short delay while qualified men were verifying the pages of maths, and while physicists were confirming that the cestron laser in the specification could be built, but at some time tomorrow the word was going to go out. The message was going to be simple: *Find Lucas Hutchman and, if he has a machine, obliterate both the man and his works.*

In the few relatively secure hours that were left to him, Hutchman had to find a good hole and crawl into it. A first consideration was that it would be a mistake to remain in Stockport, which was at the warmest end of the postal spoor he had created. The hunters would be informed that an antibomb machine would not be readily portable and could infer that, if it really existed, it was likely to be hidden somewhere in the south and not too far from Hutchman's home. They could also reason that, having traced a line towards the north of England, their quarry would be likely to double back, both to put them off the scent and to get closer to the hidden machine. That being the case, Hutchman decided on the strength of this pseudo-data, he would continue northward.

He drove up to Manchester, skirted it on the ring road,

117

and went off on a northwesterly tangent with a vague idea of trying to reach the Cumbrian lake district that night. But other considerations began to weigh on his mind. The lake district was a very long way from Hastings and it was the type of area, especially at this time of year, where the authorities would have little difficulty in controlling the exit points. It would be better to lose himself in a population centre and – if he did not want to arrive conspicuously in the dead of night – to pick one fairly near at hand. He pulled off the highway and consulted a road map.

The nearest town of any size was Bolton which, to Hutchman's mind, was the epitome of the traditionally humdrum life of provincial England. Its name produced no overtones, Freudian or otherwise, associated with Crombie-Carson's 'typical spy fantasy', which made it a good choice from Hutchman's point of view. And there was the fact that, to the best of his knowledge, not one person he knew lived there – the hunters would be likely to concentrate on areas where Hutchman was known to have friends to whom he might turn for help.

With his decision made, he got onto the Salford–Bolton road and drove with the maximum concentration on his surroundings which was becoming a habit. The easiest course would be to check in at a hotel, but presumably that would almost be the most dangerous. He needed to drop completely out of sight. Reaching Bolton, he cruised slowly until he found himself in one of the twilight areas, common to all cities and towns, where large shabby houses fought a losing battle with decay, receiving minimal aid from owners who rented out single rooms. He parked in a street of nervously rustling elms, took his empty suitcase and walked until he saw a house with a card which said 'Bed & Breakfast' hanging from the catch of a downstairs window.

The woman who answered the doorbell was in her late forties and heavy-bosomed, wearing a pink see-through blouse which covered a complexity of silk straps. Her blonde hair was elaborately piled up above a large-chinned face. A pale-faced boy of seven or eight, wearing striped pyjamas, stood close to her with his arms around her thighs.

'Good evening,' Hutchman said uncertainly. 'I'm looking for accommodation, and I saw your sign . . .'

'Oh, yes?' The woman sounded surprised to hear that she had a sign. The boy eyed Hutchman warily from the folds of her skirt.

'Have you any rooms to let?' Hutchman looked beyond her into the dimly-lit hall, with its brown linoleum and dark stairway ascending into alien upper reaches of the house, and wished he could go home.

'We have a room, but my husband usually attends to the letting and he isn't here right now.'

'That's all right,' Hutchman said with relief. 'I'll try elsewhere.'

'I think it should be all right, though. Mr Atwood will be home shortly.' She stood aside and gestured for him to enter. Hutchman went in. The floorboards creaked beneath his feet and there was a strong smell of floral air freshener.

'How long did you want to stay?' Mrs Atwood asked.

'Until . . .' Hutchman checked himself. 'A couple of weeks or so.' He went upstairs to view the room which, predictably, was on the top floor. It was small but clean, and the bed had two mattresses, which suggested it could be comfortable if a trifle high. He inquired and found that he could have full board, consisting of three meals a day, and that Mrs Atwood would take care of his laundry for a small extra charge. 'This looks fine,' he said, trying to sound enthusiastic. 'I'll take the room.'

'I'm sure you'll be very comfortable here.' Mrs Atwood touched her hair. 'All my boys are very comfortable.'

Hutchman smiled. 'I'll bring up my case.'

There was a sound outside on the landing, and the small boy came into the room carrying Hutchman's case.

'Geoffrey! You shouldn't have . . .' Mrs Atwood turned to Hutchman. 'He isn't very well, you know. Asthma.'

'It's empty,' Geoffrey asserted, nonchalantly swinging the case into the bed. 'I can carry an empty case all right, Mum.'

'Ah . . .' Hutchman met Mrs Atwood's eyes. 'It isn't completely, but most of my stuff *is* down in the car.'

She nodded. 'Do you mind paying something in advance?'

'Of course not.' Hutchman separated three five-pound notes from the roll without taking it out of his pocket and handed them to her. As soon as she had gone he locked the door, noting with surprise that the key was bent. It was a slim, uncomplicated affair with a long shaft which in the region of the bend had a bluish tinge as though the metal had been heated and bent on purpose. Shaking his head in bafflement, Hutchman threw his jacket on the bed and walked around the little room, fighting off the home-sickness which had begun to grip him again. He opened the room's only window with difficulty and put his head out. The night air was raw, making him dizzy, producing a sensation curiously similar to that in a dream of flying. His head seemed to be dissociated from his body, hovering high in the darkness close to unfamiliar arrangements of gutters and pipes, slates and sills. All around and below him lighted windows glowed, some with drawn blinds or curtains, others affording glimpses into appalling, meaningless rooms. This physical situation – his head drifting disembodied and unseen, close to the walls of a canyon of nightmare – was no stranger than the matrix of horror his life had become. He knelt that way for a long time, until the cold had eaten into his bones and he was shivering violently, then closed the window and went to bed.

The room was to be his home for the next week, and already he wondered how he could possibly survive.

11

Ed Montefiore was young enough to have begun his working life in computers; old enough to have risen to the top of his nameless section of the Ministry of Defence.

The fact that he was known – as far as anybody in his position could be known – as a computer wizard was a matter of economics rather than specialized aptitude. He had an instinct, a talent, a gift which enabled him to fix any kind of machine. It did not matter if the particular design was new to him, it did not even matter if he was unaware of the machine's purpose – if it was broken, he could lay his hands on it, commune with the ghosts of the men who had built that machine and all the others like it, and discover what was wrong. When Montefiore had found the fault he would correct it easily and quickly if he was in the mood to do so, at other times he would simply explain what needed to be done, then walk away satisfied. He had not been exercising his special ability for very long when he ceased physical repair work altogether. There was more money in finding and diagnosing faults than in putting them right.

And of all the fields in which his talents could be applied the computer business, Montefiore saw, was going to be the most lucrative. He spent several years trouble-shooting for major consultancies, jetting across the world at an hour's notice, curing computers or linked groups of computers of illnesses the resident engineering teams had been unable to deal with, accumulating money, and living like a prince between assignments.

It was just when the life was beginning to pall on

him that the Ministry made its first oblique approaches concerning the MENTOR project. As an individual, Montefiore was repelled by the idea of a vast computer complex which held in its multiple-data banks every item of information – military, social, financial, criminal, industrial – which the government needed for the control of the country's affairs. But as a man with a wild talent which demanded a new dimension of challenge he was able to throw himself into the project without reservation. He had no interest in the design or manufacturing work – MENTOR's components were relatively conventional and became remarkable only in aggregate – but keeping the huge discrete body in coordinated good health had brought something like fulfilment. It had also brought him promotion, responsibility, and a certain kind of power. No human brain could absorb more than a minute fraction of the data stored by MENTOR but Montefiore was the only man with unlimited access, and he understood how to be selective. He knew everything that was worth knowing.

The item of knowledge uppermost in his mind, as he stood at the window of his office, was that something very big was happening. An hour earlier the Minister's secretary had phoned in person with a simple message – Montefiore was to remain in his office until further contacted. There was nothing too unusual about the communication itself, but it had come through on the red telephone. Montefiore had once calculated that if his red telephone ever rang the odds would be that ICBMs would soon be climbing through the upper reaches of the atmosphere. McKenzie's words had put his mind at ease to a certain extent. They had, however, left him with a sense of foreboding.

Montefiore was of medium height, with thick muscular shoulders, and a boyish face. His chin was small, but with a set which denoted determination rather than weakness. He surveyed himself in the mirror above the white-painted fireplace and gloomily resolved to drink less beer for a few weeks, then began to wonder if the ringing of the red telephone had presaged the end of his, and everybody's, beer-drinking days. He went back to the window and was frowning down at the slow-moving tops of buses when his secretary came through on the intercom and announced that Mr McKenzie and Brigadier Finch were on their way in. Finch was head of a small group of men whose official title was the Strategic Advisory Committee and who, among other things, were empowered to advise on the pressing of certain buttons. Montefiore was not even supposed to know of Finch's connection with the SAC, and the pang of dismay the Brigadier's name inspired made him wish he had pre-served his ignorance.

The two men silently entered the room carrying metal-rimmed briefcases, shook hands with minimal formality. Both were 'clients' of MENTOR's unique information service and were well known to Montefiore. They invariably treated him with extreme courtesy but their very correctness always served to remind him that all the magics of his electronic cabal were powerless against the class barrier. He had a lower middle-class background, theirs was upper middle-class, and nothing was changed by the fact that nobody spoke of those things in the Britain of the Cockney emancipation. McKenzie, tall and florid, pointed at the randomizer switch on Montefiore's desk. Montefiore nodded and moved the switch, activating an electronic device which would prevent even an ordinary telephone from functioning properly within its field. No recordings could be made of anything that was about to be said.

'What's the problem, Gerard?' Montefiore made a

point of using Christian names, and had vowed to himself that if any of his high-level clients objected he would complete the *reductio ad absurdum* by walking out of the MENTOR project and refusing to return until his right to address Trevor as Trevor was officially ratified.

'A very serious one,' McKenzie said, taking the unusual course of staring Montefiore straight in the eye as he spoke. He opened his case, took out photocopies of some densely written pages and sketches, and set them on the desk. 'Read that.'

'All right, Gerard.' Montefiore scanned the sheets with professional speed, and his sense of imminent disaster was replaced by a strange elation. 'How much of this do you believe?'

'Believe? Belief doesn't come into it. The point is that the mathematics on those pages has been checked and verified.'

'Oh? Who by?'

'Sproale.'

Montefiore tapped his teeth thoughtfully. 'If Sproale says it's all right . . . How about the machine?' He examined the sketches again.

'Both Rawson and Vialls say the machine can be built and will . . . do what is claimed for it.'

'And the question you want me to answer, Gerard, is – has it been built?'

'We want the man who wrote this letter,' Finch said restlessly. He was a lean man, aggressively athletic for one in his fifties, and wore his dark pinstripes like a uniform. He was also, Montefiore knew, the MENTOR client with whom his familiarity rankled most.

'It amounts to the same thing, Roger.' Montefiore gave the most unmilitary salute he could devise. 'I imagine that when we find this man he'll answer all the questions put to him.'

Finch's eyes went dead. 'This is a matter of extreme urgency.'

'I get the hint, Roger.' Montefiore had been adding to his own excitement by avoiding immediate consideration of the problem, but now he began the pleasurable task of establishing parameters. 'What information have we on this man? What do we know? First of all, that he *is* a man – the handwriting makes it clear we aren't dealing with a woman, unless it's a woman who is prepared to go a long way to cover up her tracks.'

'What does that mean?' Finch made an irritated movement, as though slapping his thigh with an imaginary cane.

'A woman might have forced a man to write it all out for her, then killed him,' Montefiore said reasonably.

'Nonsense!'

'All right, Roger. You are directing me, in this national crisis, not to consider any of this country's thirty million women as a suspect?'

'Now, now, Ed,' McKenzie said, and Montefiore noted with satisfaction the use of his own Christian name. 'You know perfectly well that we never poach on your preserves. And I am sure you appreciate better than anyone else that here, in this single assignment, is the justification for every penny spent on MENTOR.'

'I know, I know.' Montefiore tired of baiting the two men as the problem claimed his mind and soul. 'The author of these papers is likely to be a male adult, in good health and vigour, if the handwriting is anything to go by – when do we get the analyst's report on the writing?'

'At any minute.'

'Good. He is also the possessor of a first-class mathematical brain. If I'm not mistaken that reduces the field from millions to thousands. And out of those thousands, one man – assuming the machine has been built – has recently spent a considerable sum of money on scientific equipment. Gas centrifuges, for instances, aren't very common devices and there's this business of using praseodymium . . .' Montefiore walked towards the door.

McKenzie started after him. 'Where are you going?'

'To the wine cellar,' Montefiore said peacefully. 'Make yourselves comfortable, gentlemen. I'll be back within the hour.'

As the high-speed elevator dropped him to bedrock level, where MENTOR's central-processing unit waited in its specially tailored and controlled environment, he felt a twinge of pity for the temporarily unknown man who had taken upon himself the role of Saviour, and who would shortly be nailed to the cross. Forty minutes later, his own act of communion completed, he braced his legs as the elevator began its climb. He glanced at the single sheet of paper in his right hand.

'You may be a good man, Lucas Hutchman,' he said aloud. 'But you're certainly a fool.'

Detective Inspector James Crombie-Carson was unhappy. He clearly remembered describing Hutchman as a walking disaster area, but he had not foreseen that the man's malign spell would encompass himself. Already he had been on the carpet before the Chief Inspector, made a butt of amusement in his own station, and had attracted the attention of the newspapers who – with their usual attention to trivia – were splashing minute details of Hutchman's escape. Now there was to be an interview with the Chief Superintendent and a faceless man from London.

'What's the holdup?' he demanded of the desk sergeant.

'I don't know, sir. The chief said he would ring when

he wanted you in.' The sergeant did not sound particularly sympathetic.

Crombie-Carson stared resentfully at the polished rosewood of the conference room door. 'Bloody waste of time! Don't they know I have other things to do?'

He paced the floor and tried to work out what had gone wrong with his career. His big mistake had been to relax his guard, to start thinking he had normal luck. The galling thing was that other men on the force casually accepted their own good luck, putting the success it brought them down to ability. There was a celebrated story that the complacent Chief Inspector Alison's first arrest had been a man who tried to reverse the charges on obscene phone calls. Crombie-Carson savoured the fable for a moment, then his thoughts were drawn back to Lucas Hutchman.

It was obvious that the man had been selling missile secrets, or preparing to do so. Crombie-Carson could recognize the type – university background, tennis and boating, married into money, too much of everything. Either had a Raffles complex, or the woman Knight had something on him. Rotten liar, too – never had the day-to-day practice that some people had to acquire just to stay alive. You could see him rearranging his scruples every time. Perhaps the Knight woman had got something really good out of him and had tried to cut herself an extra slice of cake by offering the goods elsewhere . . .

A buzzer sounded on the desk and the sergeant nodded gravely at Crombie-Carson. He took off his glasses, slipped them into his pocket, and went into the conference room where three men were seated at the long table. One of them was a watchful stranger in a dark suit.

'This is Mr Rea of . . . ah . . . the Ministry of Defence,' Alison said. 'He has come down from London to ask you some questions about the Hutchman case.'

Crombie-Carson shook hands. 'How do you do? I had an idea we might be seeing somebody from Whitehall.'

'Had you?' Rea seemed to pounce on the remark. 'What gave you the idea?'

'Hutchman works at Westfield's. A guided-missile expert and queer goings-on with a group of Communists. It seems fairly obvious . . .'

Rea looked satisfied. 'Ah, yes. Now, you interviewed Hutchman at this station for several hours, as I understand it.'

'That's correct.'

'Did he talk freely?'

Crombie-Carson frowned, trying to get the drift of the interview. 'He spoke freely, but there's the question of how much of what he said was true.'

'Quite. I expect he covered up certain things, but how did he speak about his wife?'

'It's all in the transcript,' Crombie-Carson said. 'He didn't say much about her, though.'

'Yes, I have a note of his actual words, but you were talking to him before the interrogation and you're accustomed to reading between the lines, Inspector Crombie-Carson. In your carefully considered opinion, is Mrs Hutchman involved in this affair? Apart from the marital connection, of course.'

'She isn't involved.' Crombie-Carson thought of Hutchman's smooth, tawny wife and wondered what madness had come over the man.

'You're positive?'

'I talked to Hutchman for several hours all told. And to his wife for a while. She doesn't know anything about it.'

Rea glanced at Alison and the Chief Inspector gave a barely perceptible nod. Crombie-Carson felt a flicker of gratitude. At least the old man wasn't going to let that ridiculous business with the mattress obscure twenty years of reliable service.

'All right.' Rea examined his hands, which were finely manicured but marred by sand-coloured liver spots. 'How would you say things are between Hutchman and his wife?'

'Not too good. There's this Knight woman . . .'

'No emotional ties, then.'

'I didn't say that,' Crombie-Carson said quickly. 'I got the impression they were giving each other hell.'

'Is he likely to try getting in touch with her?'

'Could be.' Crombie-Carson's eyes suddenly felt tired, but he resisted the impulse to put on his spectacles. 'He might be able to hurt her a bit more by not getting in contact, though. I'm keeping a watch on the parents' house, just in case . . .'

'We've withdrawn your men,' Chief Superintendent Tibbett said, speaking for the first time. 'Mr Rea's department has assumed responsibility for the surveillance of Mrs Hutchman.'

'Is that necessary?' Crombie-Carson allowed himself to sound offended, to demonstrate to the others that he had every confidence in his own arrangements.

Rea nodded. 'My people have more experience in this particular type of operation.'

'Well, how about the phone-tapping unit?'

'That, too. We'll handle the complete operation. You know how sensitive an area the guided-missile field is, Inspector.'

'Of course.'

When he left the conference room shortly afterwards, Crombie-Carson was pleased that Hutchman's escape had not been mentioned, but he had a peculiar conviction that the case had ramifications about which he was not being told.

12

There were several others staying in the Atwood house, but as Hutchman was the only one requiring full board he was invited to have his evening meal in the kitchen with the family. It would be much pleasanter for him, Mrs Atwood had said, than sitting alone in the dining room, which was difficult to heat anyway. Hutchman was surrounded by a swarming cloud of his own thoughts, through which the conversation of other people reached him as a semimeaningless babble. He had his doubts about the eating arrangements. After a full day in the floral-patterned room, however, the prospect of warming himself at a hearth had become more attractive. There was also the fact that he wanted to avoid behaving in a way which would appear furtive or suspicious.

He shaved his cheeks and lower lip, emphasizing his beard, and went out onto the landing. It was only when he tried to lock the bedroom door behind him that he discovered the significance of the strange bend in the shank of the key. The lock was screwed to the inner face of the door and the key, in spite of its distorted geometry, could operate it efficiently from the inside – but from the outside the key would have had to reach through the thickness of the door, and this was impossible. He could seal himself into the room, but never lock it behind him when he went out.

Subdued by a sudden insight into the way non-Hutchman minds worked on non-Hutchman planes of existence, he went down the stairs and tentatively opened the kitchen door. Warm, meaty air gusted past him from the room which was largely occupied by a table set for four. Mrs Atwood and the boy, Geoffrey, were already seated at the table, and the biggest man Hutchman had ever seen was standing with his back to a shimmering anthracite fire. His megacephalous figure was swathed in a voluminous Arran sweater which did not disguise the fact that he had the muscles of a plough-horse.

'Come in, lad,' he said in a shock wave of a voice. 'Close the door – you're letting in a draught.'

'Right.' Hutchman went in and, in the absence of introductions, decided that the giant was Mr Atwood. 'Where do I . . . ?'

'Sit here beside Geoffrey,' Mrs Atwood said. 'I like to have all my boys where I can keep an eye on them.' She uncovered a white-glass casserole dish and began spooning stew onto blue-rimmed plates. Hutchman was very much aware of the boy beside him, a tiny hominid the same size as his own son, with the quietly heaving chest of an asthma sufferer. He tried unsuccessfully to catch the child's eye.

'There you are, Mr Rattray,' Mrs Atwood said, addressing Hutchman by the name he had told her. She began to pass him a loaded plate, but her husband advanced from the fireplace.

'That's not enough to line a man's stomach,' he boomed. 'Give him some more, Jane.'

Hutchman reached for the plate. 'No, this is more than enough, thanks.'

'Nonsense!' Atwood's voice was so loud that Hutchman actually felt the table reverberate under his hand. He saw the boy beside him flinch. 'Pay no attention to him, Jane. Fill that plate.'

'I assure you . . .' Hutchman stopped speaking as he saw the pleading expression on Mrs Atwood's face, and allowed her to heap more of the thick stew on top of the ample portion she had already served.

'Get that down you. Build you up a bit.' Atwood accepted his own mountain of food and began eating it with a soup spoon. 'You eat yours up too, Geoffrey.'

'Yes, Dad,' the boy said compliantly and began to eat.

A silence fell over the room, broken only by what sounded to Hutchman like the roar of a distant crowd and which he identified a moment later as coming from Geoffrey's chest. The boy seemed disturbed by his father and Hutchman tried to visualize how the giant must appear through a seven-year-old's eyes. Enormous, terrifying, incomprehensible. During the soundless day in the bedroom he had passed some time by trying to adopt other people's viewpoints and had found the experience unsettling. There was, for instance, the question of marital infidelity. Even in the final quarter of the twentieth century most men – *I should know* – were devastated to discover that their wives had been unfaithful; but how could a man ever appreciate the woman's point of view? Supposing the situation were reversed and women were the sexual predators? How long would the average man hold out if an attractive woman came pestering him to go to bed with her, pushing and pleading, refusing to take no for an answer? He realized that Atwood had spoken his temporarily adopted name.

'I beg your pardon.'

Atwood sighed heavily, hugely. 'I said, what do you do, lad? For a living?'

'At the moment, nothing.' Hutchman had not expected to be quizzed, and spoke coldly to ward off any further questions.

'But when you're doing something, what is the something you do?' Atwood appeared not to notice he had been snubbed.

'Ah . . . I'm a designer.'

'Hats? Knickers?' Atwood gave a pleased guffaw.

Hutchman realized he had chosen too exotic a profession. 'No. Steel-framed buildings. I'm more what you might call a draughtsman.'

Atwood looked impressed. 'Good job, that. Plenty of work for draftsmen in these parts.'

'Yes – that's why I'm here. I'm going to take it easy for a few days, then have a look around.' Hutchman felt he had woven an acceptable story.

'I'm a greengrocer, myself,' Atwood said. 'Do you take a sup?'

'Beer? Sometimes.'

'Good. As soon as you've finished that we're going down to the Cricketers for a few pots of ale.'

'Thanks, but I think I'd prefer not to have a drink this evening.'

'Nonsense,' Atwood bellowed. 'I'm not talking about that southern piss. We're going to have some good Lancashire ale.' He directed a fierce look at Hutchman's plate, which was still almost full. 'Get that into you, lad. No wonder you're so skinny . . .'

'That's enough, George,' Mrs Atwood snapped. 'Remember Mr Rattray's a guest in this house.'

'Hold your tongue!' Atwood scowled at her, his massive chin jutting. 'Isn't that why I'm inviting him to have a drink?'

Hutchman felt the boy move uneasily beside him, his breathing becoming noisier. 'It's all right, Mrs Atwood. I can see that your husband is being hospitable, and on second thought maybe I should go out for an hour.'

Atwood nodded. 'That's more like it. Now finish your supper, lad.'

Hutchman met his gaze squarely as he pushed the plate away. 'If I eat a lot, I can't drink afterwards.'

When the meal was over he went up to his room, put on his jacket, and looked out into the night. It had begun to rain and the tiny segments of rooms floating in the darkness seemed more dismal than they had on the previous night. George Atwood was a hulking lout, an insensitive animal who dominated others by his sheer size, but an evening in his company would be better than an evening alone in the room with the advancing floral walls. *Vicky*, the thought came against his will, *look what you've brought me to.*

He went back downstairs, walked into the kitchen, and saw his own face on the screen of the television set in the corner. Jane Atwood was watching a news programme, with her back turned towards the door, and she did not see him enter the room. He left without being heard and waited in the dimly-lit hall for George Atwood to appear. The news bulletin was substantially the same as the one he had heard in the car while driving north – which might be an indication that he had been connected with the antibomb machine. He had provided the authorities with a good, publicly acceptable reason for hunting him down. They would be able to use every communication medium to the limit, and only a few people might stop to wonder why a mere witness in an abduction case was receiving so much prominence. The photograph being broadcast was hauntingly familiar to Hutchman, with its mottled background suggestive of foliage, but he could not remember where it had been taken or who had held the camera. No doubt all his friends and acquaintances had been questioned by the police and possibly by men from some nameless branch of the security machine. *Was* it possible? Hutchman counted the hours – this was Tuesday evening and the Britain-bound envelopes had not been posted until Monday.

It's too soon, Hutchman decided, relaxing slightly after

the uneasy experience of seeing himself on the screen. *I can cope with the police, and the others still have no idea who it is they have to hunt.*

'Right, lad!' Atwood bustled out of another door, wearing a hairy coat which gave him bearlike proportions. His sparse locks had been slicked down across his enormous skull with water. 'Where's your car?'

'Car?' Hutchman had parked his car on a cindery patch at the side of the house, and had been planning to leave it there.

'It's raining out there, lad.' Atwood spoke with ponderous exactitude. 'My van is out of action and the Cricketers is a good half-mile from here. If you think I'm going to walk it in the rain, think again.'

Hutchman, needled by the other man's unvarying boorishness, was tempted to call the expedition off, but reminded himself that the car no longer fitted the broadcast description. It would, in any case, be no more noticeable in a pub car-park than sitting virtually on its own beside the house.

'My car's just outside the door,' he said. They ran to it in chilling rain. Atwood jigged impatiently until Hutchman opened a door for him, then he threw himself into the seat with an impact that rocked the car on its suspension. He slammed the door with similar violence, making Hutchman wince.

'Let's go,' Atwood shouted. 'We're wasting good drinking time.'

As he started up the engine Hutchman tried to recapture the odd craving for pints of stout which had gripped him on Sunday night on the way to Crymchurch police station, but all that happened was that he got a cold feeling in his stomach. With Atwood directing, he drove out to the main road, the blue-white lighting of which emphasized the drabness of the buildings, and along it for a short distance to an unimpressive red-brick inn. Hutchman surveyed the place gloomily as he got out of the car. On every past occasion when he had become involved with a dedicated beer drinker and been dragged off to the area's reputed sole source of good ale the pub concerned had always turned out to be remarkably dismal. This one was no exception to what apparently was a natural law. As they ran to the entrance through the rain he experienced a sad conviction that it was a warm starry night far to the south in Crymchurch. *I'm lonely without you, Vicky . . .*

'Two pints of special,' Atwood called to a barman as soon as they got inside the public bar.

'Make that a pint and a whisky,' Hutchman said. 'A double.'

Atwood raised his eyebrows and parodied Hutchman's home-counties accent. 'Ho, pardon flipping me! If you wants whisky, Trevah, you can flipping well pay for it.' He leaned on the dark wood of the counter, shaking with amusement, then doggedly pursued his joke. 'Ay'm reduced to common beastly beer this month – pater has cut may allowance, you see.'

Giving way to his annoyance, Hutchman took the thick roll from his pocket and threw a five-pound note onto the counter without speaking. When his drink came he drained the glass. The liquid warmed his stomach immediately, then seemed to follow an anatomically impossible radiant course into the rest of his body. During the following two hours he drank fairly steadily, paying for most of the rounds, while Atwood engaged the barman in a long, repetitive dialogue on football and greyhound racing. Hutchman wished for someone to talk to, but the barman was a tattooed youth who viewed him with scarcely veiled hostility; and the only other customers

137

were silent, raincoated men who sat on bench seats in darker recesses of the room.

Why is everybody doing this? He was filled with a dull wonder. *Why are they all here, doing this?*

There was a doorway behind the counter which led into the select bar, and through it Hutchman caught brief glimpses of a queenly barmaid. She seemed to laugh a lot, gliding easily through the cozy orange light of the other room. Hutchman prayed for her to come and talk to him, vowing he would even refrain from looking down her blouse if she would only lean on his part of the bar and talk to him and make him feel partly human again. But she never entered the public bar and Hutchman, absurdly, was trapped with Atwood. As his loneliness grew, the familiar lines from Sassoon returned with almost unbearable poignance . . . *and tawdry music and cigars, I oft-times dream of garden nights, and elm trees nodding at the stars* . . . his throat closed painfully . . . *I dream of a small fire-lit room, and yellow candles burning straight, and glowing pictures in the gloom, and friendly books that hold me late* . . .

Sometime later the young barman drifted away to other company and Atwood, after a disappointed look around the room, decided to focus his conversation on Hutchman. 'Good paying job, a draughtsman's, isn't it?'

'Not bad.'

'What's the screw?'

'Ten thousand,' Hutchman guessed.

'What's that a week? Two hundred. Not bad. Does it cost much to get a boy in?'

'How do you mean?'

'I read that when a kid's going to be an architect his folks have to put so much . . .'

'That's architecture.' Hutchman wished the barman

would return. 'A draughtsman serves an ordinary apprenticeship so it wouldn't cost you anything.'

'That's all right then.' Atwood looked relieved. 'Happen I might put young Geoff into being a draughtsman.'

'Supposing he doesn't like It?'

Atwood laughed. 'He'll like it all right. He can't draw very well though. The other day he tried to draw a tree – and you should've seen what he did! All whirls and squiggles it was. Nothing like a tree! So I showed him the right way and – give the lad credit – I must say he picked it up right fast.'

'I suppose you showed him how to do a comic-book tree?' Hutchman dipped his finger into a spot of beer and drew two straight parallel lines surmounted by a fluffy ball. 'Like that?'

'Yes.' A suspicious look passed over Atwood's slablike face. 'Why?'

'You fool,' Hutchman said with alcoholic sincerity. 'Do you know what you've done? Your Geoffrey, your only child, looked at a tree and then he put his impressions of it down on paper without reference to any of the conventions or preconceptions which prevent most human beings from seeing *anything* properly.' He paused for breath and, to his surprise, saw that he was getting through to the big man.

'Your boy brought you this . . . holy offering, this treasure, the product of his unsullied mind. And what did you do, George? You laughed at it and told him that the only way to draw a tree was the way the tired hacks who work for the *Dandy* and the *Beano* do it. Do you know that your boy will never again be able to look at a tree and see it as it really is? Do you realize he might have been another Picasso if – '

'Who d'you think you're kidding?' Atwood demanded,

but his eyes were clouded with genuine concern. Hutchman was tempted to confess he had only been playing with words, but the giant was discovering that his privacy had been invaded by a stranger and he was growing angry. 'What the hell do you know about it, anyway?'

'A great deal.' Hutchman tried to be enigmatic. 'Believe me, George, I know a great deal about such things.' *I'm the ground zero man. Didn't you know?*

'Get stuffed.' Atwood turned his head away.

'Brilliant,' Hutchman said sadly. 'Brilliant repartee, George. I'm going ho . . . to bed.'

'Go ahead. I'm staying on.'

'Please yourself.' Hutchman walked to the door with unnatural steadiness. *I'm not drunk, officer. Look! I can crawl a straight line.* It had stopped raining, but the air outside was much colder than before. An icy, invisible torrent flooded around him, robbing his body of heat. He took a deep breath and launched himself through the darkness in the direction of his car.

There were only four vehicles in the parking lot, but it took Hutchman a considerable time to accept the simple fact that his car was not among them.

It had been stolen.

13

Muriel Burnley was going through a new and very unsatisfactory phase of her life.

She had never been happy working for Mr Hutchman, with his thoughtlessness, and his disregard for company regulations, a disregard which caused her endless work of which he was not even aware. As Muriel drove to the office in her pale-green Morris Mini she added to the catalogue of things she had disliked about Mr Hutchman. There was his casual attitude about money – which was all right for somebody who had married into it, but not all right for a girl who had to help support her home on a secretary's salary. Mr Hutchman had never inquired about her mother's poor state of health, in fact – Muriel stabbed her foot down on the accelerator – Mr Hutchman probably did not even know she had a mother. She had made the biggest mistake of her career when she had allowed the personnel officer to assign her to Mr Hutchman. The trouble was that, shameful admission, in the days when she had seen him only from a distance she had been impressed by his resemblance to a young Gregory Peck. That sort of look was unfashionable now, of course, but she had heard that Mr Hutchman often had trouble with his marriage and, as she worked so closely with him in the office, there had been a possibility that . . .

Appalled by where her thoughts were leading, Muriel urged her car forward, overtook a bus, and got back into lane just in time to avoid a van travelling in the opposite direction. She compressed her lips and tried to concentrate on the road.

And to think that all the time Mr High-and-mighty Hutchman had been carrying on behind his wife's back with that tart in the Jeavons Institute! It had been obvious that something was going on, of course. Mr Batterbee had gone the same way, but even filthy Mr Batterbee hadn't got himself involved with underworld characters and brought the police snooping around the office. Muriel's face warmed as she remembered the closeted interviews with the detectives. The other girls had been delighted, naturally. They talked a lot in the corridors in small gleeful groups which fell strangely silent when she approached. It was obvious what they were thinking, of course. Mr Hutchman had turned out to be a . . . whoremaster, and Muriel Burnley was his secretary, and the police weren't paying all that attention to our Muriel for nothing . . .

She swung the car past Westfield's security kiosk and braked with unnecessary abruptness in the parking lot. Gathering up her basket, she got out, locked the doors carefully, and hurried into the building. She walked quickly along the corridors without meeting anybody, but on rounding the corner nearest her own office she almost collided with Mr Boswell, head of Missile R and D.

'Ah, Miss Burnley,' he said. 'Just the person I wanted to see.' His blue eyes examined her interestedly through gold-rimmed spectacles.

Muriel drew her coat tighter. 'Yes, Mr Boswell?'

'Mr Cuddy has been seconded to us from Aerodynamics, and he will be taking over Mr Hutchman's duties today. He's going to have a lot on his plate for a few weeks and I want you to give him all the co-operation you can.'

'Of course, Mr Boswell.' Mr Cuddy was a small dry individual, who was also a lay preacher. He was sufficiently respectable to counteract Mr Hutchman's aura to some extent.

'He'll be moving his things over this morning. Will you fix up the office before he arrives? Get him off to a good start, eh?'

'Yes, Mr Boswell.' Muriel went to her office, hung up her coat, and began tidying the larger adjoining room. The police had spent a full morning in it and, although they had made some attempt to put everything right before leaving, had created an air of disorder. In particular, the desk's oddments tray, where Mr Hutchman kept an astonishing number of paper clips and pencil stubs, had been left in a hopeless jumble. Muriel slid the tray out of its runners and emptied it into a metal wastebin. Several pencil ends, clips, and a green eraser fell wide and bounced across the floor. She gathered them up and was about to dispose of them when she saw something printed in ink on the side of the eraser. The words were: '31 CHANNING WAYE, HASTINGS.'

Muriel carried the eraser into her own office and sat down, staring nervously at it. The detective who interviewed her had returned again and again to the one line of questioning. Had Mr Hutchman another address, apart from the one in Crymchurch? Had he an address book? Had she ever seen an address written on any of his waste paper?

They had made her promise to contact them if she remembered anything that even seemed like an address. And now she had found what their careful search had missed. What did the Hastings address represent? Muriel tightened her grip around the piece of India rubber, digging her fingernails into its pliant surface. Was this the place where Mr High-and-mighty had gone when he was with that whore who disappeared? Had he been in Hastings with her all those days last month?

143

She lifted the telephone, then set it down again. If she called the police her involvement with those awful detectives would begin all over, and her so-called friends along the corridor had had enough fun at her expense already. Even the neighbours were looking at her strangely. It was a miracle that none of them had seized the chance to upset her mother with their gossip – but why should Mr High-and-mighty be shielded? Perhaps he was hiding in Hastings at this minute.

Muriel was still struggling to reach a decision when a furtive sound from next door told her that Mr Spain had arrived, late as usual. She stood up and smoothed her blouse down over her breasts time after time before carrying the eraser into his office.

Every time Don Spain accidentally met or saw a person he knew, he made a mental note of the time and the day and the place. He did this instinctively, without any conscious effort and for no other reason than that he was Don Spain. The information was filed and never forgotten, because sometimes a piece of knowledge which was uninteresting in itself became very important when joined to another equally insignificant scrap acquired perhaps years earlier or later. Spain rarely tried to turn his stores of information to any advantage, or to use them in any way. He simply did what he had to do, with no recompense other than the secret thrill he occasionally received when – perhaps out for an evening drive – he glimpsed an acquaintance on the road and was able to deduce his destination, reason for going, and other relevant circumstances. Spain fancied that a portion of his own consciousness detached itself on such occasions and travelled away with the acquaintance, diffusing his worldline over many other lives.

Thus it was that, although he had never actually spoken

to Vicky Hutchman, he had a fair degree of certainty that she would be walking through the arcade from Crymchurch High Street at approximately ten o'clock on Wednesday morning. There was an expensive beauty salon at the end of the arcade, where she had a weekly appointment, and from what Spain knew of Mrs Hutchman she was not a woman to allow little things like a shattered marriage and a disappearing husband to interfere with the rites of self-preservation. He glanced at his watch, wondering how long he could afford to wait if she did not arrive on schedule. Maxwell, the chief accountant, had been making himself objectionable for some time with pointed remarks about the inadvisability of trying to serve two masters. Settling the score with Hutchman was important but not worth losing money over, which would be the case if he provoked a clampdown and was forced to give up some of his outside work.

Spain cleared his throat as he saw Vicky Hutchman approaching. He judged his moment, then stepped out of the doorway where he had been waiting and collided with her.

'Excuse me,' he said. 'Why . . . it's Mrs Hutchman, isn't it?'

'Yes.' She looked down at him with ill-concealed distaste, in a way which reminded him of her husband, strengthening his resolve. 'I'm afraid . . .'

'Donald Spain.' He cleared his throat again. 'I'm a friend of Hutch's. From the office, you know.'

'Oh?' Mrs Hutchman looked unconvinced.

'Yes.' *She's just like big Hutch*, Spain thought. *He wouldn't sully himself with ordinary people, either – except when he thought nobody was looking.* 'I just wanted to say how sorry everybody is about the trouble he's in. There must be a simple explanation . . .'

'Thank you. Now if you'll forgive me, Mr Spain, I have

an appointment.' She began to move away, her blonde hair smooth as ice in the watered-down, railway station light of the arcade.

It was time to strike. 'The police haven't found him yet, I see. I think you did the right thing in not telling them about your summer cottage. That's probably . . .'

'Summer cottage?' Her brow wrinkled slightly. 'We have no cottage.'

'The one in Hastings – 31 Channing Waye, isn't it? I remember the address because Hutch asked my advice about the lease.'

'Channing Waye,' she said in a faint voice. 'We have no cottage there.'

'But . . .' Spain smiled. 'Of course – I've said too much already. Don't worry, Mrs Hutchman. I didn't mention it to the police when they interviewed me, and I won't mention it to anyone else. We all think too much of Hutch to let . . .' He allowed his voice to tail off as Mrs Hutchman hurried into the crowd, and when he turned away he was filled with a pleasant, scoured-out feeling, as though he had just written a poem.

Nothing has changed, Vicky Hutchman told herself as she lay back in the big chair and the warm water flowed downward across her scalp. *The nortriptyline will help. Dr Swanson says the nortriptyline will help if I only give it time to build up in my system. The past is really the past . . .*

She closed her eyes and told herself she could not hear the beginnings of that thin, sad song.

14

Beaton had been born in the town of Oradea, near the northwest border of Rumania, the son of a pottery worker. His name for the first thirty-two years of his life had been Vladimir Khaikin, but he had been known as Clive Beaton for a long time now and his original name sounded foreign even to his own ears. He had joined the army at an early age, worked hard, and shown certain aptitudes and attitudes which brought him to the attention of a discreet organization known, in some places, as the LKV. The offer of employment he received was sufficiently interesting for him to agree to quit the army while still a captain, and to disappear from normal life while he was being retrained. At that point his new career became less exciting and less glamorous – he had found himself spending a lot of time observing the activities of tourists and visiting Western businessmen. Khaikin was becoming thoroughly bored when a door, not to a new career, but to an entirely new life swung open.

It happened when a coach full of British tourists went off the road and smashed its way down a hillside less than a hundred kilometers from his hometown. Some of the party were killed instantly and a few died later in hospital from burns. As is customary in such cases, the LKV ran a thorough check on all the dead and – as only occasionally happens – they found one victim who was worth resurrecting. He was Clive Beaton, age thirty-one; unmarried, no close relatives, occupation – postage-stamp dealer, hometown – Salford, Lancashire. The LKV then went through their files of members who were cleared for unlimited service and came up with one whose height, build, and colouring matched those of the dead man.

Khaikin had no hesitation in accepting the assignment, even when he learned that a certain amount of plastic surgery would be performed on him and that some of it would simulate heat scars on his face. He spent three weeks in an isolated room in the hospital, while surgeons supposedly fought to restore his ravaged face. This period gave the surgeons a chance to simulate severe injuries without actually destroying facial tissue, but it was more valuable to the LKV who used the time for an intensive study of Clive Beaton's background, friends, and habits. Every scrap of information they garnered was memorized by Khaikin, and a voice coach overlaid his standard English with a Lancashire accent. Khaikin's retentive mind absorbed everything without effort and when he was flown to London, and eventually reached Salford, he settled into his new life in a matter of days. There were times during the following years when he almost wished that some difficulty would arise to exercise and test him, but there were compensations, among them – absolute freedom.

The LKV made few demands beyond requiring him to live in obscurity as Clive Beaton, to be in England, and to wait. He allowed the stamp dealership to die a natural death and devoted himself to other pursuits to which his instincts were more attuned. His native love of horses, coupled with a flair for probability maths, led him into the penumbra of occupations surrounding the turf. He gambled successfully, worked as a private handicapper for several small stables, and opened his own book when betting shops became legal. This was something he would have done earlier but for the fact that one of his prime directives forbade any conflict with authority. Once established as a bookmaker he attracted, almost against his will, a wide range of associations with men who lived beyond the law; but Beaton never set a foot across the finely drawn line. Although he thought of himself as Clive Beaton, although he had learned to like Scotch whisky and English beer, he never married – and he never answered a telephone without half-expecting to hear a voice from the past.

The special calls came very rarely. Once, when he had been in England about two years, the nameless caller – who was identified by code only – instructed him to kill a man who lived at a given address in Liverpool. Beaton had found the man, who looked like a retired sailor, and had knifed him the same night in a dark street. Back in Salford, he had read all the papers carefully, but the police seemed to be treating the affair as a simple dockland stabbing; it quickly faded from the regional news and there were no repercussions of any kind. Beaton wondered afterwards if the killing had had no motive other than the checking of his own efficiency and loyalty, but such thoughts troubled him infrequently. In general the sort of assignments he received, at roughly yearly intervals, reminded him of his old tourist-watching days – tasks like making sure that a given individual really was staying at a given hotel.

The Hutchman case, however, had all the portents of a major job right from the start. It had begun a day earlier with a notification of a high priority number, a statement that Hutchman was considered a focus of 'continuing interest', and an instruction to place himself on round-the-clock standby. Since then Beaton had not strayed more than a few paces from his private telephone.

The voice, when it came, sounded both urgent and grim.

'Mr Beaton,' it said, 'I'm a friend of Steel's. He asked me to call you about the outstanding account.'

Beaton acknowledged the code by responding with his own credentials. 'I'm sorry I haven't paid – can you send me another statement?'

'This is ultimate priority,' the voice said without preamble. 'You have been following the news about the disappearance of the mathematician, Lucas Hutchman?'

'Yes.' Beaton listened to all news broadcasts very carefully, and a less sensitive ear than his would have picked up its undertones. 'I know about him.'

'Hutchman is believed to be in your area and his papers must be transferred to folio seven immediately. Is that clear?'

'Yes.' Beaton felt cold and excited at the same time. He had, for the first time in many years, been instructed to kill another human being.

'Folio seven. *Immediately*. We have no exact location for him, but we picked up a police radio report that a black Ford Sierra had been found abandoned between Bolton and Salford in Gorton Road.'

'Wasn't Hutchman driving a blue – ?'

'The police reported that the car did not match the description on the tax disc. The disc said blue.'

'That's all very well, but if Hutchman has abandoned the car he certainly won't have stayed in the vicinity. I mean . . .'

'We believe the car was stolen from him, and then dumped.'

An alarming thought struck Beaton. 'Just a minute. We're discussing this very openly on the phone. Supposing somebody's listening? What happens to my cover?'

'Your cover is no longer important.' The urgency in the voice had been replaced by a raw edge of panic. 'There is no time to arrange meeting places and private talks. All efforts must be devoted to the Hutchman transfer. We are sending every available man, but you are the closest and must take what steps you can. This is ultimate priority – do you understand?'

'I understand.' Beaton set the phone down and walked across his apartment to a mirror. He was not the same man who had come to England. His hair was grey now, and the years of good living had thickened and softened his body. More dismaying was the abrupt realization that the years had also softened his thinking – he did not want to hurt anybody, or to kill anybody. And yet, what would an ideal be worth unless one was prepared to serve it? And what would life itself be worth without an ideal to bring some meaning to the endless alternation of pleasure and pain? Beaton removed a cloth-wrapped bundle from the recess behind a drawer in his writing table. From it he took a well-oiled automatic pistol, a clip of 9-mm. cartridges, a tubular silencer, and a black-handled switch-blade knife. He assembled the pistol, slipped it into an inside pocket, put on his overcoat, and went out with the closed knife growing warm in his right hand.

It was early in the afternoon and a blue-grey mist was veiling the more distant buildings. The sun could be stared at without discomfort, a disc of electrum, slowly falling. Beaton got into his Jaguar and drove towards Bolton. Fifteen minutes later he parked in a narrow street and walked up an alley. It was not raining but there was enough moisture in the air to make the paving stones glisten blackly. Near the end of the alley he opened a small door and went through it into a cavernous brick building which had once been stables and now served as a garage. A mechanic looked up from the engine of an elderly sedan and eyed him incuriously.

Beaton nodded. 'Is Raphoe in?'

'In the office.'

Beaton walked across the oil-blackened floor and up a stair to where a boxlike office clung to the ancient wall.

Paraffin fumes gusted hotly around him as he opened the door. A fat man with a pendulous strawberry nose was seated at a desk in the office.

'Hello, Clive,' he said resentfully. 'That was some horse you gave me for Friday.'

Beaton shrugged. 'If you could pick winners every time there'd be no books.'

'So I hear, but I don't take to the idea of my money being used to push up the odds on the real trier.'

'You don't think I'd do that to you, Randy.'

'Not much, I don't. Are you going to give me my hundred notes back?' Raphoe sneered.

'No, but I've one for Devon and Exeter on Saturday which is already over the line.' Beaton watched and saw the predictable flicker of interest in Raphoe's eyes.

'How much?'

'The syndicate is charging me the odds of two thousand on this one, and that's a lot of money to lay off, but you can have it free, Randy.'

'Free!' Raphoe gently pressed the end of his ruinous nose, as though hoping to mould it into a more conventional shape. 'What's the catch?'

'No catch.' Beaton made it sound casual. 'I just want to know where your boys picked up the black Ford Sierra they dumped in Gorton Road.'

'I knew it!' Raphoe slapped his desk gleefully. 'I knew that one was radioactive as soon as Fred drove it through that gate. As soon as I saw the bum paint job and the brand-new plates I said to Fred, "Get that heap out of here and bury it." I said to him, "Never nick a car that somebody else has just nicked."'

'You told him the right thing, Randy. Where did he pick it up?'

'You say this horse is over the line?' Raphoe asked significantly.

152

'Master Auckland II,' Beaton said, giving a genuine tip. Raphoe was a notorious loudmouth, and giving him the information would set up a chain reaction of tip-offs which would bring the odds tumbling down and cost Beaton a considerable sum of money. He had an intuition, however, that he was not going to be worried about horses in the immediate future.

'It'll be really trying, will it?'

'Randy, this time it doesn't need to try. Now, about the car – where did you get it?'

'In the car park of the Cricketers. Do you know it? It's a good alehouse out Breightmet way.'

'I'll find it,' Beaton assured him, and now the knife seemed to be generating a pulsing warmth of its own, bathing his palm with sweat.

15

Hutchman rarely recalled his dreams, with the result that when he did awaken with one fresh in his mind it seemed – although he was sceptical about precognition – to be laden with significance and psychological implications. His last remembered dreams were the two about the timid pseudo-creatures who allowed themselves to be destroyed by women. (*Am I,* he had wondered, *a shaky artificial being which falls apart at the hands of female pragmatism?*) Now, however, he had the unusual experience of expecting a dream, of knowing in advance that one was coming. It was something to do with the increasing sense of being trapped in the shabby old house, or the feeling of imminent disaster which had haunted him since his car had vanished, which by a kind of transference made the dinginess of his surroundings seem menacing. As he lay down on top of the bedclothes on a grey afternoon, there was danger for him in the ancient brown bakelite of the room's electrical fittings, despair in the shattered skeletal elements of the gas fire. And the dream came . . .

He walks downstairs, oppressed by the gloomy unfamiliarity of the house. There is a wedding party in progress down below and the stairwell is filled with hostile northern accents. George Atwood's voice swells and recedes with an undersea quality. There is a painful pressure in Hutchman's bladder which must be relieved. He tries the two toilets and the doors are locked. The pressure gets worse. Afraid of disgracing himself, he asks Mrs Atwood if there is another toilet. Not here, she says, but the house next

154

door is empty. Hutchman hurries out to it. The street is filled with bright pewter light, and the worn sandstone steps of the abandoned house register vividly in his mind. The front door is lying open. Dust is drifting on the bare, rotting boards of the hall as he walks along it. There is an open door to the room on his left. He looks in and sees, lying on a couch, a figure completely covered by a white sheet. Dread grips him, but the toilet is only at the head of the first flight of stairs and the pain in his abdomen is intolerable. He walks up the stairs, opens the toilet door, and finds himself staring down into an old cast-iron bath. There is a corpse in it – yellowed, frilled with fungus, bathed in the fluids of its own putrefaction. Appalled, Hutchman sways ponderously away and turns to run. But now the front door of the house is closed. And, projecting from the inner doorway he had passed, is the corner of a white sheet. The thing which had been lying on the couch is now standing in the entrance to the front room, waiting for him to come downstairs. And even if he gets past it in full flight, while he is struggling to open the outer door it will come up behind him. Hutchman tries to scream. *Run! Stay! Run! Stay!*

It was still daylight when he awoke but the room seemed very much colder than before. He lay flat on his back, hands gripping the bedding as if to prevent him from falling upward while he fought off the spell of the nightmare. It had been a very basic affair, he told himself. Hammer Films stuff, and utterly ridiculous to a waking adult; but the room was undeniably colder. He got to his feet, shivering, and turned up the gas fire, causing a white front of incandescence to move up through its ruined ceramic temples, followed by bands of violet and sienna.

Run! Stay!

Perhaps he should have pulled up stakes as soon as his

car was stolen. It might have been best to have got going immediately, not even returning to the house for the night. But he had been drunk at the time, and rapidly becoming sick, and it had seemed that the thief had done him a good turn by removing a troublesome piece of unwanted property. Now he was uncertain, and glands which had been triggered by his dream were urging him to run. He left his room and wandered slowly down the stairs, pausing at different levels in the structure as though he could and might decide to move horizontally through the air at any one of them. A woman's voice floated up the stairwell. It was Jane Atwood speaking to someone on the telephone, cheerful, privileged to communicate with her friends outside. Hutchman felt a pang of loneliness, and he decided to ring Vicky. *It's possible*, he thought in wonder. *I can pick up the phone and speak to her. Dial a line to the past.* He moved on down to the hall, where Mrs Atwood was hanging up the phone.

'That was George,' she said curiously. 'A man's been to the shop asking about you. Something about your car.'

'Really?' Hutchman gripped the smooth wood of the banister.

'Was your car stolen, Mr Rattray? You said it broke down when you were . . .'

'I'm not sure – it may have been stolen afterwards.' Hutchman turned and sprinted up the stairs, moaning inwardly with panic. In his room he threw on his jacket and ran back down to the hall. Mrs Atwood had disappeared into another part of the house. He opened the front door and glanced up and down the street to make sure nobody was coming, then walked quickly away from the house, choosing to go in the opposite direction to the main road. Near the end of the street he saw a dark-blue Jaguar sweep round the corner. It was driven by a thick-set, grey-haired man who appeared not even to see

Hutchman, but the car slowed down at once and rolled gently down the street, its wheels mushing through decaying leaves. The driver was examining the numbers on the houses.

Hutchman continued walking normally until he had rounded the corner into a wider and empty cross-avenue, then began to run. The act of running required no effort, his breath seeming to come easier as though constrictive bands had been torn away from his chest. He sped along a line of trees, hardly aware of his feet touching the ground, moving so silently that he twice distinguished the pulpy sound of chestnuts dropping onto the pavement. Near the end of the avenue he abruptly became self-conscious, slowed down to a walk, and looked back over his shoulder. The blue Jaguar was backing out between the lines of trees, wallowing slightly with the lateral forces of the turn. It came in his direction, alternating through light and shade as it ghosted past the trees.

Hutchman began to run again. He emerged into a long canyon of three-storey terrace houses, saw a narrow street opening on his right, and darted down it. This street was freakishly long and featureless, running slightly uphill until its perspectives faded into the gathering mist. There was no time for Hutchman to turn back. He loped along an irregular line of parked cars, zig-zagging to avoid groups of playing children, but now running was becoming less dreamlike and more difficult. His mouth began to fill with a salty froth and his ankles to weaken, allowing his feet to slap the ground almost uncontrollably. He looked back and saw the Jaguar in its noiseless pursuit.

Suddenly Hutchman noticed a ragged break in the confining lines of houses. He slanted towards it and entered a desolate plain which had been created by a slum clearance and redevelopment programme. Its surface was composed of tumbled brick and fragmented concrete, with children moving through a low-lying mist, like members of a small alien race, bands of expeditionary Hobbits. Hutchman launched himself in the direction of the opposite boundary, another row of terrace houses beyond which the blue-white lights of a main road were already beginning to shine through the dusk. Behind him he heard the Jaguar slither to a halt. Its door slammed, but ther was no time for him to take even one glance to the rear because running on the new surface was dangerous. His ankles threatened to give way every time he was forced to leap over a block of concrete or one of the rusted reinforcing rods which rose out of the ground like snares. He aimed for what appeared to be an opening in the perimeter houses, then discovered he had wasted his strength by running. The redevelopment contractor had sealed the site off with a galvanized iron fence – and Hutchman was in a box.

He turned with the absurd idea of trying to mingle with a group of urchins but, using the well-developed instincts of their race, they had faded into the surroundings. The grey-haired man was only fifty paces away, running strongly in spite of his bulk, looking strangely incongruous in an expensive tweed overcoat. He was carrying a slim-bladed knife in a way which suggested he knew how to use it.

Sobbing, Hutchman moved to one side. His pursuer altered course to intercept him. Hutchman lifted a half-brick and threw it, but had aimed too low and it struck the ground harmlessly. The grey-haired man jumped over it, landed awkwardly and pitched forward, his face driving into a thicket of steel rods which projected from a slab of concrete. One of them punched its way into the socket of his right eye. And he screamed.

Hutchman watched in horror as a surprisingly large

158

white ball, blotched with red, sprang from the socket and rolled on the ground.

'My eye! Oh God, my eye!' The man grovelled in the dirt, his hands searching blindly.

'Stay away from me,' Hutchman mumbled.

'But it's my eye!' The man got to his feet with the obscene object cupped in his hands, holding it out towards Hutchman in a kind of supplication. Deltas of black blood spilled down his face and over his clothes.

'Stay away!' Hutchman forced his body into action. He ran parallel to the fence for a short distance and angled away towards the point where he had entered the site. Children darted out of his path like startled pheasants. He reached the blue Jaguar and got into the driving seat, but there was no ignition key. His pursuer had been taking no chances. Hutchman got out of the car as several children appeared in the gap in the houses. They were going back into the site, but moving differently, with an air of authority which suggested they had the backing of adults. Hutchman hurried towards the street and encountered two middle-aged men, one of them in slippers and rolled-up shirt-sleeves.

'There's been an accident,' he called, pointing back across the desolation to where a single figure wavered in the slate-coloured mist. 'Where's the nearest telephone?'

One of the men pointed to the left, down the hill. Hutchman ran in that direction, back the way he had come, until he was in the wider tree-lined avenue. He slowed to a walk, partly to avoid looking conspicuous and partly because he was exhausted. The easier pace also made it possible for him to think. He had a feeling the man he had encountered was not a British detective or security agent – it would all have been handled differently – but no matter how much anybody might

159

have learned from Andrea Knight, how could they possibly have found him so quickly? There was the car, of course, but surely that would have brought the police down on him rather than an anonymous man carrying a knife. Regardless of what had happened, he decided, Bolton was no longer safe for him.

As his breathing returned to normal Hutchman reached the main road and caught a bus going into the town centre. Darkness was falling by the time he got off near the imposing town hall. Store windows were brightly lit and the pavements were crowded with people hurrying home from work. The crisp, pre-Christmas atmosphere brought on another of the unmanning attacks of nostalgia and he found himself thinking about Vicky and David again. *Look what you've done to me, Vicky.*

He asked a news vendor how to reach the railway station, set out to walk to it, then realized he could not risk going to any transport terminal, and that to consider it had been a dangerous lapse. *I wanted to ride home in comfort, sitting in a window seat, humming 'Beyond the Blue Horizon'*, he thought in astonishment. *But I'm the ground zero man, and I can never go home again.*

He walked aimlessly for a while, twice turning into side streets when he saw police uniforms. The problem of getting out of Bolton was doubly urgent. Not only had he to escape from a tightening net, but the deadline he had given to the authorities was drawing closer. He had to journey south and be in Hastings before Antibomb Day. Could he travel in disguise? A flash recollection of Chesterton's invisible man caused him to halt momentarily. The uniform of a postman would make him effectively invisible, and a rural postman's traditional transport – a bicycle – would probably get him to Hastings in time. But how did one acquire such things? Stealing them would only serve to make him more easily identifiable . . .

In one of the narrow side streets he saw the yellow electric sign of a taxi company, and in the window of the office beneath it was a notice which said: 'DRIVERS FOR SAFETY CABS WANTED – NO PSV LICENCE REQUIRED.'

Hutchman's heart began to thud as he read the hand-lettered card. A taxi driver was just as invisible as a postman, and a vehicle went with the job! He walked into the dim-lit garage beside the office. A row of mustard-coloured taxis brooded in the half-light and the only evidence of life was the glowing window of a boxlike office in one corner. He tapped the door and opened it. Inside was a cluttered room containing a table and a bench upon which sat two men in mechanic's overalls. One of them was in the act of raising a cup of tea to his mouth.

'Sorry to disturb you.' Hutchman put on his best grin. 'How do I go about getting a job as a driver?'

'No trouble about that, mate.' The mechanic turned to his companion, who was unwrapping sandwiches. 'Who's the super tonight?'

'Old Oliver.'

'Wait here and I'll fetch him,' the mechanic said in a friendly tone and went out through a door which led to the back of the building. Encouraged and gratified, Hutchman studied the little room as he waited. The walls were covered with notices held in place by drawing pins and yellowing Sellotape. 'Any driver who is involved in a front-end accident will be dismissed immediately,' one stated. 'The following are in bad standing and must not be accepted for credit card journeys,' said another above a list of names. To Hutchman, in his state of intense loneliness, they appeared as indications of a warm, intensely human normalcy. He entertained fantasies of working contentedly in a place like this for the rest of his life if he got away from Hastings in one piece. Getting his job, being accepted into the cheery incident-rich life of a cab driver, assumed an illogical and emotional importance which had nothing to do with escaping to the south.

'Cold day,' the remaining mechanic said through a mouthful of bread.

'Certainly is.'

'Fancy a drop of tea?'

'No thanks.' Hutchman's eyes stung with pleasure as he refused the offer. He turned as the door opened and the first mechanic came in accompanied by a stooped, white-haired man of about sixty. The newcomer was pink-faced, had a prim womanly mouth, and was wearing an old-fashioned belted raincoat and a peaked cap.

'Hello,' Hutchman ventured. 'I understand you have openings for drivers.'

'Happen I have,' Oliver said. 'Come out here and I'll talk to you.' He led the way out to the garage area and closed the office door so that the mechanics would not hear the conversation. 'Are you a PSV man?'

'No, but it said on your notice that . . .'

'I know what it said on the notice,' Oliver interrupted pettishly, 'but that doesn't mean we don't prefer good professional men. These nasty little so-called safety cars with seats looking out the back window have cheapened the whole trade. Cheap and nasty.'

'Oh.' It dawned on Hutchman that he was dealing with a man who regarded taxi-driving as a calling. 'Well, I have a clean ordinary licence.'

Oliver scrutinized him doubtfully. 'Part-timer?'

'Yes – or full-time. Whatever you want.' Hutchman wondered if he sounded too anxious. 'You do need drivers, don't you?'

'We don't pay a wage, you know. You get a third of

your take, plus tips. A good man does well out of tips, but a beginner . . .'

'That sounds fine. I could start right away.'

'Just a minute,' Oliver said sternly. 'Do you know the town?'

'Yes.' Hutchman's heart sank. How could he have forgotten one of the basic requirements?

'How would you get to Crompton Avenue?'

'Ah . . .' Hutchman tried to remember the name of the main road he had driven along with Atwood, the only one he knew. 'Straight out to Breightmet.'

Oliver nodded with some reluctance. 'How would you get to Bridgeworth Close?'

'That's a tricky one.' Hutchman forced a smile. 'It might take me some time to get to know *all* the streets.'

'How would you get to Mason Street?' Oliver's womanly lips were pursed in disapproval.

'Is that out towards Salford? Look, I told you . . .'

'I'm sorry, son. You just haven't a good enough memory for this kind of work.'

Hutchman gazed at him in helpless anger, then turned away. Outside, he stared resentfully at the unfamiliar configurations of buildings. He had been rejected. His brain held information which was going to change the entire course of history, but a prissy old fool had looked down on him because he wasn't familiar with a haphazard pattern of streets in an indistinguished . . . *Pattern!* That's all it was. A man did not have to grow up in a town to get to know its layout if he had the right sort of mental disciplines.

Glancing at his watch, Hutchman found it was only a little after 5:30. He hurried to the nearest main thorough-fare, located a large stationery store, and bought two street maps of Bolton and a white correcting pencil. While he was paying for them he asked the sales assistant

163

where he could find a copying service still open. The girl directed him to a place two blocks further along the same street. He thanked her, went outside, and shouldered his way through the crowds, reaching the office-equipment supplier, who did copying, just as an unseen clock was chiming the hour. A dapper young man with wispy fair hair was locking the door. He shook his head when Hutchman tried the handle. Hutchman took two five-pound notes from his pocket and pushed them through the low-level letter slot. The young man picked them up cautiously, studied Hutchman through the glass for a second, then opened the door a little.

'We close at six, you know.' He held the notes out tentatively.

'Those are yours,' Hutchman told him.

'What for?'

'Overtime payment. I have an urgent copying job which must be done right now. I'll pay for it separately, but that tenner's for you – if you'll do the work.'

'Oh! Oh, well then. You'd better come in.' The youth gave a baffled laugh and opened the door wide. 'Christmas is early this year, I must say.'

Hutchman unfolded one of his street maps. 'Can you handle a sheet this size?'

'With ease.' The youth activated a grey machine and watched with perplexity as Hutchman took out the typist's correcting pencil and, working at careless speed, obliterated all the street names. When he had finished he handed the map over. 'Do me . . . mmm . . . a dozen copies of that.'

'Yes, sir.' The young man stared solemnly at Hutchman as he worked.

'I'm in advertising,' Hutchman said. 'This is for a market-research project.'

Ten minutes later he was back out on the street with a

warm roll of sheets under his arm. He now had all the equipment needed to carry out the type of memory blitz he had perfected in his university days, but there was still the problem of finding a quiet and secure place in which to work. The soothing effect of constructive activity abated slightly as it came to him that he was going to a great deal of trouble to get out of Bolton without having checked that it was really necessary. He saw a small newsagent's shop on the opposite side of the street and crossed over to it. While still in the middle of the roadway he read the billboard which was leaning against a window sill.

It said: 'POLICE CORDON SEALS OFF BOLTON!'

A number of copies of the evening paper were clipped to a wire rack in the doorway. He approached the shop and saw that a large photograph of himself was featured on the front page, with splash headlines which read: 'BOLTON SURROUNDED BY POLICE CORDON. Mystery mathematician traced here today.' Hutchman decided not to risk going in and buying a paper – he had learned all he needed, anyway. He was turning away from the shop when a white Porsche drew up beside him and the passenger door was pushed open. The driver was an Oriental-looking girl in a silver dress.

'It's warmer at my place,' she said, showing no trace of embarrassment over the fact that she sounded exactly the way a prostitute was supposed to sound.

Hutchman, who had been poised to flee, shook his head instinctively then caught the edge of the door. 'Perhaps I *am* a little cold.' He got into the car, which smelled of leather and perfume, and was accelerated smoothly and expensively into the clustered lights of the town centre.

He turned sideways to face the girl. 'Where are we going?'

'Not far.'

Hutchman nodded contentedly. He was satisfied as long as she did not try to take him out of town, through a roadblock. 'Have you any food at your place?'

'No.'

'Aren't you hungry?'

'Starving – but I don't run a soup kitchen.' Her neat face was hard.

Hutchman snorted, took a ten-pound note from his pocket, and dropped it on her lap. 'Stop at a take-away and get us some food.'

'I'm a working girl, mister.' She flicked the note back at him. 'The rate is exactly the same for companionship.'

'That's understood – your name isn't Melina Mercouri. How much for the night?'

'A hundred.' Her voice was defiant.

'A hundred it is.' Hutchman peeled off ten more notes, amazed at the fact that they still held value for other people. 'Here's the hundred, *plus* the food money. All right?'

For an answer she put her hand on his thigh and slid it into his crotch. He endured her touch without speaking. *I could kill you, Vicky.* The girl stopped at a snack bar, ran into it, and emerged with an armful of packages which smelt of roast chicken. She drove him to a small apartment block about ten minutes from the town centre. Hutchman carried the food while she let herself in, and they went to a first-floor flat. It was simply furnished with white walls, white carpet, and a black ceiling in the main room.

'Food first?' the girl said.

'Food first.' Hutchman spread the packages on the table, opened them, and began to eat while his hostess was making coffee in a clinically bright kitchen. He was tired and nervous – pictures of a human eye rolling in the

166

dust flickered before him – but the heat was helping him to relax. They ate in near silence and the girl cleared the remains into the kitchen. On her way back she slipped out of the silver dress with a single lithe movement, revealing that she was wearing a crimson satin bikini suit which, along with a certain muscularity of thighs, gave her the air of a trapeze artist. Her spice-coloured body was trim and taut and desirable. Hutchman's groin turned to ice.

'Listen,' he said, lifting his roll of ammonia-smelling sheets. 'I have some very urgent business to attend to for my firm, and I won't be able to relax until it's out of the way. Why don't you watch television for a while?'

'I haven't got television.'

Hutchman realized he had made a mistake in suggesting it – he was bound to be in the news more than ever. 'Play music or read a book, then. All right?'

'All right.' The girl shrugged unconcernedly and, without dressing again, lay down on a couch and watched him.

Hutchman spread out a street map, the one which still showed the names, and began memorizing it, starting with the major roads and filling in as much as possible on side streets. He worked with maximum concentration for one hour, then took a blank copy, and tried filling in the names. This gave him an accurate indication of the areas in which he was doing well and of the ones – still a great majority at this stage – where his performance was poor. He returned to the named map, spent a second hour on it, did another progress check with a blank map, and started the process all over again. Sometime during the course of the evening the girl fell asleep and began snoring gently. She woke with a start around midnight, gazing at Hutchman without recognition for an instant.

He smiled at her. 'This is taking longer than I expected. Why don't you go to bed?'

'Do you want coffee?'

'No, thanks.'

The girl got to her feet, shivering, gathered her silver dress from the floor and walked into the bedroom with a curious glance at his array of maps. Hutchman went back to work. It was almost three o'clock by the time he finally managed to fill in a complete map, and by then he too was shivering. The central heating had been off for hours. He lay down on the couch and tried to sleep, but the room was becoming intensely cold and his head was bursting with hundreds of street names. Each time he closed his eyes he saw networks of black lines, and occasionally a red-blotched eye rolled across them. After half an hour he went into the bedroom. The girl was asleep in the centre of an outsize bed. Hutchman undressed, got in beside her, and placed one hand on her up-thrust hip, feeling the edge of the pelvic basin and the belly warmth under his fingertips. In that respect, in the darkness, she could have been Vicky.

He fell asleep instantly.

At the first light of morning he got up without disturbing the girl, dressing quickly, and went back to the table in the main room. As he had expected, when he tried to fill in a map there were several new areas of uncertainty. He spent several minutes revising them and quietly left the apartment. It was a grey, dry morning, surprisingly mild for the time of year. He decided to walk into the town centre, amusing himself as he went by accurately predicting the names of the streets he reached. The crammed knowledge of the town's layout was of the most transient kind and would be virtually gone inside a week, but he would have it long enough to get him through any quiz which might take place that morning. He reached the taxi company's headquarters without seeing any police. This time he went into the outer office and spoke to a bespectacled girl who had several telephones and a microphone on her desk.

'Is Oliver on duty?'

'No – he's on the late shift this week. Was it personal?'

Hutchman was encouraged. 'No, not personal. I'm a good driver and I know Bolton like the back of my hand . . .'

Forty minutes later he had been issued with a 'uniform', which consisted of an engraved steel-lapel badge and a peaked cap, and was cruising through the town in a mustard-coloured taxi. For the best part of an hour he genuinely worked as a cabdriver, making two pickups to which he was directed by radio and locating the destinations without much difficulty. The second one left him on the south side of the town and instead of returning to his waiting station he radioed the office.

'This is Walter Russell,' he said, using the name with which he had signed on. 'I've just picked up a gentleman who wants to spend the day touring the countryside around Bolton. What's the procedure?'

'The daily rate is forty pounds,' the girl replied. 'Payable in advance. Is that satisfactory to your customer?'

Hutchman waited a moment. 'He says that's fine.'

'All right – call in when you are free again.'

'Right.' Hutchman replaced the microphone. Having decided that the limited-speed taxicab might look out of place on the motorways, he drove due south for Warrington with the intention of travelling down England on the more homely linking roads. A short distance ahead of him he saw three teenage girls standing at the roadside thumbing a ride. They glanced at each other in consternation when he pulled up beside them and operated the lever which opened the passenger door.

'Where are you heading for?' he called, trying to sound benevolent in spite of his growing tension over the road-block he sensed must be close by.

'Birmingham,' one of the girls said, 'but we've no money for a taxi.'

'You don't need money for this taxi.'

'What do you need, then?' another girl demanded, and her companions giggled.

Oh, God, Hutchman thought. 'Look, I'm going down to Ringway Airport to meet a customer. I offered you the free seats, but if you don't want them that's all right with me.' He made as if to close the door and the girls screamed and tumbled into the aft-facing seats. When the car was moving again they talked among themselves as though Hutchman did not exist, and he gathered they were on their way to a Damascus demonstration. He discovered, with a dull sense of surprise, that he had not thought about Damascus for days. That he no longer really cared about the ruined city and its indomitable seven-year-olds who would never see eight. It was a personal thing now. A triangle. Vicky and he and the antimbomb machine.

There was a lengthy queue of cars at the police road-block, but the uniformed men glanced only once at the taxi and its occupants, and signalled Hutchman to drive on.

16

It was past midnight when Hutchman got off the train in Hastings.

He had brought the little car south to Swindon, which was as close to his destination as he dared bring an obvious trail-marker, and had abandoned it in an untended taxi rank during the afternoon. From there he had taken a train to Southampton and another along the coast to Hastings, but the connections had worked out badly and the rest of the day had been spanned by periods of nervous waiting and incredibly slow travel.

His knowledge that there were now less than thirty-six hours to go until the deadline weighed heavily on him as he emerged from the station on to a sloping forecourt. The grey mildness of the morning had given way to a clean, cold rain which threshed noisily in the gutters, and which soaked Hutchman almost as soon as he stepped into it. Several taxis were waiting, but he decided that they represented too big a risk. He slipped past them in the shadows and set out to walk to Channing Waye. The journey took fifteen minutes and by the time he reached the house he was as wet as if he had fallen into the sea, and was shivering uncontrollably.

He opened the front door of the dark little house but paused before going in, gripped by a strange timidity. This was the penultimate point of no return, barely less final than the pressing of the black button itself. He had no subconscious yearning to be deflected from his course by an outside agency – his life had become so twisted and deformed that turning back would have been the only act less meaningful than going on. But once he went into the house, once he was swallowed by the dankness of the cramped hall and had closed the door, he would have severed all links with humanity. Even if he was traced to the house and men tried to break in, their only achievement would be to make him press the button a little earlier. He was the ground zero man, and he was committed . . .

The door was swollen with moisture and he had to use his shoulder to get it closed properly. He found his way upstairs by the vague radiance which seeped in through the transom from a streetlamp. Nothing happened when he tried the light but he was able to discern that the room had not been interfered with in his absence. It still contained its single bentwood chair, painted gooseberry green, and the components of his machine. He stumbled back down to the hall in squelching shoes, located a main electrical switch under the stairs, and turned it on. Hampered by the clinging coldness of his clothes, he backed out of the cubbyhole and went through all the rooms, putting on the lights and closing the blinds. The total effect was to make his tiny domain more bleak and depressing than before. He went out to the covered backyard, where the rain fretted against a glass roof, and looked into the concrete coal bunker. It contained barely enough fragments to fill a bucket, and no shovel. He cast around the yard, found some worn oilcloth on the floor of the outside lavatory, and used it to scoop up the coal and carry it to the fireplace in the back room. Being virtually a non-smoker, Hutchman had no lighter but he was able to light a piece of newspaper at the self-igniting gas stove in the kitchen. The oilcloth burned greasily, with a whirring sound, and even when supplemented with twists of newspaper would not trigger off the coals. He hesitated then, amazed at the tenacity of his inhibitions,

172

took the wooden drawer from the kitchen table, smashed it underfoot, and fed it to the fire. This time the coals ignited, guaranteeing him a meagre ration of heat for perhaps an hour.

He stripped off all his clothes and wrapped himself in the only material available, which was the loose covering of a large sofa, and settled down to wait for thirty-five hours. *I dream of a small fire-lit room*, he thought. And this time the tears came easily.

When Hutchman awoke in the morning he had a pounding headache and a raw sensation in the back of his throat. Each breath he drew was a torrent of icy air ripping through his nasal passages. He sat up painfully and surveyed the room. The fireplace held nothing more than a handful of grey ash, and his clothes were still damp. Trying to suppress his shivering, he gathered up the wrinkled garments and carried them into the kitchen. He lit the oven of the cooker and all four burners, then force-dried his clothes, absorbing as much heat as possible into his body in the process. As he waited he developed a powerful craving for tea. Not the delicate Darjeeling he used to drink with Vicky – but strong, cheap, pensioner's tea, served hot and sweet. A conviction stole over him that a pot of such tea would cure his headache, soothe his throat, and drive the pains from his joints. He searched the kitchen cupboards, but his unknown landlord had left nothing at all in them.

All right, he thought. *If there's no tea in the house, I'll go round the corner and buy some.*

The idea filled him with a childish, feverish delight. He had sworn not to open the front door until after he had fulfilled his mission in case there were watchers outside, but surely that was being too cautious. If he had been followed this far he would have known about it by now.

He dressed quickly, savouring the bonus the new decision had brought him. It would be good to walk into an old-fashioned grocery, just as any other human being could, and smell the hams and the fresh bread. It would be so good to go through the commonplace human actions of buying tea and milk and sugar . . .

'Stands the church clock at ten to three?' he said aloud, in a stranger's voice. 'And is there honey still for tea?'

He pulled on his grey jacket and was walking to the door when he glimpsed himself in the hall mirror. His hair was matted down across a bearded face which was a death mask of Christ. He was red-eyed, dirty, rumpled, ill – and strange. Above all, he looked strange, a spectre which could not fail to draw the attention of a friendly old grocer or anybody else who saw him even for a moment. There could be no question of his leaving the house.

'Is it a party in a parlour?' he demanded, bemusedly, of himself. '. . . some sipping punch, some sipping tea; But, as you by their faces see, All silent and all *damned!*' The walls swayed towards him.

He walked upstairs towards his machine, and was surprised when he fell near the top and had to cling to the banister. *I'm ill*, he thought. *I really am ill.* The discovery brought with it a yammering fear that he might not be able to assemble the machine properly, or not be conscious to activate it at the appointed time. He squared his shoulders, went into the rear bedroom, and began to work.

Reality came and went at intervals during the course of the day.

At times his hands seemed to work quite capably by themselves, effortlessly checking the power pack and carrying out the highly precise task of setting up the laser and aligning the optical coupling. Offsetting this was the

174

fact that other parts of the work which he had expected to complete with ease became dismayingly difficult. The aiming tube for the output ray, for example, was controlled by a clockwork motor and a gearing system which kept it pointing in the direction of the moon – the natural reflector Hutchman had chosen to disperse the radiation efficiently across the globe. His hands took care of the basic setting up of this section but when he opened the almanack he had included with the machine to get co-ordinates for the moon's movements, the figures were near-meaningless jumbles. His concentration on them was marred by bouts of weakness, lapses when he could think of nothing but hot tea, and dreamlike spells when he visited the dappled landscape of the past. Vicky refusing to be consoled after a quarrel: 'When people are angry they sometimes say things they really mean.' Walking with her in Bond Street when on the opposite pavement a woman opened an umbrella, a point of red which blossomed into a circle on one side of Hutchman's vision, simulating the approach of a missile and causing him to duck instinctively and to understand – for the first time – why umbrellas should not be opened near horses. David falling asleep in his arms, wondering aloud: 'Why does a one and a nought mean ten, and two ones mean eleven instead of a one and a nought meaning eleven and two ones meaning ten?' Vicky scolding him: 'Why don't I believe in Oxfam? Listen, when eleven million children die every year there's no point in raising funds – the entire history of the planet is working against you.' Sipping whisky while the poplars darkened against the sunset . . .

With the machine assembled, the rest of the day passed more quickly than Hutchman had expected. He moved an armchair into the tiny kitchen and huddled close to the cooker, with his feet actually inside the oven. His feverishness and the gassy fug in the airless room encouraged him to doze, to skip in and out of real time. The dreams were clear, warm pools of remembrance in which he drifted at ease over the varicoloured shingles of the past, selecting and examining events as a diver picks up brilliant pebbles and lets them tumble slowly from his grasp. Sometime after midnight the dry pain in his throat dragged him upwards into consciousness. He eased it with warm water heated in an old jam jar which had been lying in the corner of the yard, and tried to sleep again.

The obtruding knowledge that there were now less than twelve hours to go made it difficult. There was also the niggling realization that he should leave the vicinity of the cooker and go upstairs to the machine where there was less chance of his being overcome by a surprise attack. But if he went up there, he rationalized, he would be cold and might succumb to the illness which was racking his body. Foetus-folded into the chair, wrapped in stained linen, he tried to visualize the increasing tempo of activities to which he had driven other men.

The search would be at its height, of course, but that was no longer so important because now that he had reached the machine he was going to make it do its work, before the deadline if necessary. More vital was what must be happening at all those secret places across the globe where nuclear arms were stored. Hutchman was suddenly struck by the vastness of his own presumption. He knew absolutely nothing of the practical detail design of H-bombs – supposing that in his theoretician's sublime ignorance he had not allowed enough time for the warheads to be broken down into sufficiently sub-critical concentrations? Even if he had given ample warning for technicians working in normal circumstances, what would happen in a Polaris submarine cruising below the Arctic icecap? And was it possible that a power which had been considering a nuclear attack against a hostile neighbour would be prompted to act while there was still time?

In the morning he got painfully to his feet, frightened by the sound of his own breathing, and drank some more warm water. He looked at his watch. Less than three hours to go. Supporting himself against the wall and then on the banister, Hutchman went upstairs and sat on the pale-green chair. He leaned sideways and threw the switches which put the machine in a state of readiness, then he made sure his hand would fall easily and naturally on to the black button.

He was ready.

He closed his eyes and waited, smiling at his vision of Vicky's face when she finally understood.

The sound of a metallic crash in the street outside shocked him into wakefulness. He sat absolutely motionless, finger on the button, and listened. In a few seconds there came the familiar ringing of high heels on pavement – a woman's footsteps, running – followed by a pounding on the door of the house. Still Hutchman refused to move, to be tricked into taking his finger away from the button.

'Lucas,' a voice called faintly. 'Lucas!'

It was Vicky.

Transported to new levels of fear, Hutchman ran drunkenly down the narrow stairs, and wrenched open the front door. Vicky was standing there. Her face flowed like molten wax when she saw him.

'Get away,' he shouted. 'Get away from here!' He looked past her and saw that two cars had collided at the corner of the street. Men in dark suits and overcoats were running.

'Oh God, Lucas. What's happened to you?' The colour had left Vicky's face.

Hutchman snatched her into the hall and slammed the

door shut. Dragging her with him, he ran up the stairs, into the back bedroom, and dropped into his chair.

'Why did you come here?' He spoke between the harsh roars of his breathing. 'Why did you have to come here?'

'But you're alone.' Vicky spoke faintly as her uncomprehending eyes took in the bare room. 'And you're ill!'

'I'm all right,' he said inanely.

'Have you *seen* yourself?' Vicky covered her face and began to cry. 'Oh, Lucas, what have you done to us?'

Hutchman gathered up the old sofa cover and pulled it tighter around his shoulders. 'All right, I'll tell you. But you must listen carefully and you must believe – because there isn't much time.'

Vicky nodded, her face still hidden in gloved hands.

'What I've done is build this machine.' He spoke sadly, with the rich compassion he could afford now that Vicky was about to come to her moment of truth. 'And when I turn it on – as I'm going to do at noon today – every nuclear bomb in the world will explode. *That's* what I was doing when you thought . . .' His voice faded as Vicky opened her hands and he saw her face.

'You're *mad*,' she whispered strickenly. 'You really have gone mad!'

Hutchman pushed the matted hair away from his forehead. 'Don't you understand *yet*? Why do you think they're hunting me? Why do you think the whole world is hunting me?' He pointed towards the street with a dirt-streaked hand.

'You're ill,' Vicky announced with the crisp determination he knew so well. 'And you need help.'

'No, Vicky, no!'

She turned and ran for the stairs. Hutchman lunged for her, tripped on his improvised shawl, and went down on his side. He got to the top of the stairs just as Vicky was reaching the front door.

178

She pulled it open and ran straight into two of the dark-suited men.

One was carrying a heavy pistol. He pushed Vicky aside, and Hutchman watched the foreshortening of his arm without realizing it meant the pistol was being aimed at him. Vicky clawed the man's face. The other dark figure spun her round and drove a karate blow into her neck. Even from the top of the stairs Hutchman heard the crushing of bone. He put his foot on the top step as the pistol unleashed its thunder, and his arm went dead. The floor of the landing ballooned up and hit him. He scuttled, whimpering, into the rear bedroom and got his finger on to the black button.

Keeping it there, he twisted himself upward until he was sitting on the chair and facing the door.

And when the two men entered the room he was smiling.

17

'Move away from the machine,' said the man with the pistol. His long face was grey, priestly with implicit purpose.

'Gladly.' Vicky was dead, Hutchman knew, but he was strangely unmoved. Sensation was returning to his numbed arm, and now he could feel blood streaming over his fingers. 'But are you sure you want me to move away from it?'

'Don't play games. Stand clear!'

Hutchman smiled again, feeling his lips crack. 'All right, but have you noticed where my finger is?'

'I can put a bullet through your solar plexus before you can move your finger,' the big man assured him earnestly. 'Then you won't be able to press that button.'

'Perhaps you can.' Hutchman shrugged. The only effect Vicky's death had had so far was to make his mind feel *cold*. His thought processes had a cryogenic rapidity. 'But you are missing my point. Look really closely at my finger, and you'll see . . .'

'*He's already pressed it!*' The man who had broken Vicky's neck spoke for the first time. '*Let's get out of here. They'll be here any second.*'

'Hold on.' The bigger man appeared suspicious of Hutchman's calmness, and personally affronted by it. He aimed the pistol squarely at Hutchman's stomach. 'What happens if I call your bluff – with a bullet?'

'You'll be doing your masters a disservice.' Hutchman almost laughed – the man was trying to scare him with a gun, not knowing that with Vicky dead there was no longer any meaning to words like fear, hatred, or love.

'You see, I'm a weak man, and when I was building this machine I had to make allowances for my own character defects. I anticipated that a scene like this one might occur – so I designed the trigger circuits so that they will function when I take my finger *off* this button.'

The big man stared in bafflement, a muscle twitching at the corner of his mouth. 'I could wreck the machine.'

Hutchman coughed so painfully that he half-expected to feel blood in his throat. 'In three seconds? That's all it will take for the output radiation to get to the moon and back – and besides to do that you'd have to force me to hold the button down. And I assure you I'll release it if you take one step into this room.'

'Give it up,' the other man said anxiously to his companion. 'Come on, for God's sake! I think I hear somebody . . .'

There was the sound of the front door of the house being thrown open and shuddering against the wall. The bigger man turned away from Hutchman, raising his pistol. Hutchman's flow of sense impressions was blasted and disrupted for an indeterminate time by the sound of machine guns being fired in a confined space. The two men disappeared from his view in a cloud of smoke, dust, and whirling flakes of plaster – then there was silence. A few seconds later he glimpsed khaki uniforms on the landing, and two soldiers in battle kit came into the room. Without speaking they took up positions on each side of the doorway and covered Hutchman with weapons which were still belching acrid smoke.

He sat without moving as the room gradually filled with other men, most of them in civilian clothes. They stared reverently at Hutchman, their eyes taking in every detail of his appearance and of the machine he was touching, but nobody spoke. Out in the street a siren wailed briefly and died away in a disappointed moan. Hutchman watched the strangers, dreamily aware that the situation had its ludicrous aspects, but his arm was throbbing hotly now and he had to concentrate hard to keep from fainting. He looked down at his watch. The time was three minutes before noon.

Close enough, he thought. *Three minutes won't make any difference. But* . . . The trouble was that he could not let go and take his rest just yet. He had specified a noon deadline, and at least one invariant point had to remain – otherwise nothing he had done could retain its meaning.

A stocky, grey-haired man entered the room, and somebody closed the door behind him. The latest arrival was expensively tailored and the conservative cut of his clothes contrasted strangely with his hard, swarthy face, which could have belonged to a Mexican bandit. Hutchman identified him and nodded tiredly in welcome.

'Do you know me, Hutchman?' he said, without preamble. 'I'm Sir Morton Baptiste, Her Majesty's Minister of Defence.'

'I know you.'

'Good. Then you understand I have the authority to have you executed right now, this *instant*, if you don't move away from that machine.'

Hutchman looked down at his watch. *Two minutes.* 'There's no need to have me killed, Minister. I'll move away from it now if you want.'

'Then do so.'

'Don't you want to know, first, why the two men who got here before you didn't kill me?'

'I . . .' Baptiste looked at Hutchman's finger on the button, and his brown eyes died. 'You mean – ?'

'Yes.' Hutchman was impressed with the speed at which Baptiste's mind had assessed the situation. 'It's a dead man's hand device. It will work when I take my finger off the button.'

'The power supplies,' Baptiste snapped, glancing around the room. One of the men who had come in with him shook his head slightly.

'Self-contained,' Hutchman said. 'About the only thing which could stop me now is if another country can drop a nuclear bomb on Hastings within the next ninety seconds.'

The nameless man who had shaken his head in answer to Baptiste's previous question about the power supplies came forward and whispered something in the Minister's ear. Baptiste nodded and made a signal which prompted someone to open the door.

'If you have just received some scientific advice about shifting the machine's position, say with machine-gun fire, don't try to follow it,' Hutchman said. 'It's good advice – shifting the machine would cause the output ray to miss the moon – but if anybody tries to leave the room or to get out of the line of fire, I take my finger off the button.'

He checked the time again. *One minute.*

Baptiste approached him. 'Is there any point in appealing to your loyalty?'

'Loyalty to what?'

'To your . . .' Baptiste hesitated. 'You didn't give us enough time, you know. At this moment your own countrymen are working on nuclear warheads, trying to dismantle them in time. And if you activate that machine . . .'

'Tough,' Hutchman commented. *Vicky is already dead.*

'You *fool*!' Baptiste struck Hutchman across the mouth. 'You're an *academic*, Hutchman. A theoretician perched on an ivory tower. Don't you see you're achieving precisely nothing? Don't you see – ?'

'It's too late,' Hutchman said, raising his hand in absolution. 'I've done it.'

Epilogue

Happiness, like many other things, is a question of relativity – of a reasonable compromise between ambition and ability. And in a way the three of us have achieved contentment.

I have just finished bathing Vicky and putting her to bed. No, she wasn't killed that day in Hastings, although her neck was broken and the doctors tell me it is a miracle she survived. The paralysis is permanent, they say, but we are making progress in other directions – with drugs for example – and her incontinence is being brought under control. I don't mind feeding her and attending to small matters of hygiene, and – although Vicky won't admit it – she finds an odd fulfilment in being able, legitimately, to occupy virtually every moment of my every day. In this mood of honesty, I should admit that, while I would give the earth to see her walk again, part of me rests easier in the long cool nights beside this new Vicky who is so . . . tractable. We no longer have those ghastly attritive arguments on subjects which only the old Vicky could have conceived, subjects such as the underlying psychological reasons for my referring to a dress which zips up the back as a dress which zips down the back.

The authorities have been kind. This 'establishment' is just the sort of place I had been expecting. It *is* right in the heart of 'The Avengers' country, but there is a village not very far away where David goes to school. His progress is much better than at Crymchurch, although Vicky swears it is because I devote much more time to him now. Possibly this is true. The authorities have provided me with a certain amount of work in my own field, but it seems to be as much an occupational therapy as anything else, and I'm never forced to burn the midnight oil.

For my own part, I cannot describe myself as unhappy. I have my small fire-lit room, and only occasionally am I disturbed by thoughts of the events of that October and November. It was a near-miracle that only a handful of tactical nuclear weapons still had their warheads intact when neutrons began to dance, and that nobody was killed when they detonated. Nobody I know of, that is. The biggest question hanging over that period is: Would I still have released the button if Baptiste had advanced his last argument first?

There is no doubt that I *was* everything he said – a fool, an academic, a theoretician. And, as he explained to me afterwards (when it was too late), the outcome of my efforts had been a temporary but incredibly expensive check in the arms race. Nuclear weapons were not discarded, as I had so myopically expected. They were simply redesigned to allow for the possibility of a Hutchman Trigger being in existence. The classical nuclear device with two fissionable masses, one of them very close to critical, has had to be abandoned in favour of a new arrangement of up to a dozen sub-critical masses which are brought together by servomechanisms when the missile is over its target. If these new weapons are ever used, and if one of my beloved machines is in operation somewhere in the world, the warheads will detonate perhaps a tenth of a second too early. But with the megaton ranges which are popular these days, a tenth of a second is neither here nor there.

This, then, was the sum total of my achievement – that I diverted many billions of any currency unit you care to mention into an unnecessary detour in the arms race. How many human lives does that represent in terms of hospitals not built, of aid programmes cancelled, of food and medical supplies never shipped? How many withered babies have been buried in shoe boxes because of me?

I don't know.

Furthermore, I never try to work it out – as I would have done in the old days. You see, I learned many things during my visit to ground zero, and one of them was that Vicky had been right all along. Nature never designed a nervous system which could withstand the burden of guilt we can apply to ourselves by feeling responsible for the actions of others. A successful species is numerous – for the precise reason that the premature death of a proportion of its members will not materially affect the welfare of the greater number. It is in obedience to a cosmic principle that a quail flying south to the sun still enjoys its little life to the full, in spite of the fact that some migrants have been snared by peasants' nets.

As Vicky might have put it: 'What sin is there in living the life you would have lived before communications within the global village became too good?'

At times a small, obdurate part of my soul whispers an uncomfortable answer to that question, but I am not disturbed. Having been to ground zero and back I can counter that one easily and finally.

What's the use? I ask the walls of my small fire-lit room. *What is the use of trying?*

The world's greatest science fiction authors
now available in paperback from Grafton Books

Samuel R Delaney
Stars in My Pocket Like Grains of Sand   £2.50   ☐

William Gibson
Neuromancer   £2.50   ☐

Sterling E Lanier
Menace Under Marswood   £1.95   ☐
The Unforsaken Hiero   £2.50   ☐
Hiero's Journey   £2.50   ☐

Ian Watson
Chekhov's Journey   £1.95   ☐
The Book of the River   £1.95   ☐
The Book of the Stars   £2.50   ☐

To order direct from the publisher just tick the titles you want
and fill in the order form.   **SF1382**

Fantasy authors in paperback from Grafton Books

Raymond E Feist
Magician   £2.95 ☐

Richard Ford
Quest for the Faradawn   £2.50 ☐
Melvaig's Vision   £2.50 ☐

Robert Holdstock
Mythago Wood   £2.50 ☐

Michael Shea
Nifft the Lean   £2.50 ☐
A Quest for Simbilis   £1.95 ☐

Tim Powers
The Anubis Gates   £2.95 ☐

To order direct from the publisher just tick the titles you want
and fill in the order form.   **SF1482**

The world's greatest science fiction authors now available in paperback from Grafton Books

Bob Shaw

The Ceres Solution	£1.50	☐
A Better Mantrap	£1.50	☐
Orbitsville	£1.95	☐
Orbitsville Departure	£1.95	☐
Fire Pattern	£1.95	☐
The Palace of Eternity	£2.50	☐

Arthur C Clarke

1984: Spring (non-fiction)	£2.50	☐
The Sentinel	£2.95	☐
2010 Odyssey Two	£1.95	☐

Harry Harrison

West of Eden	£2.50	☐
Skyfall	£2.50	☐
Captive Universe	£1.50	☐
You Can be the Stainless Steel Rat: An Interactive Game Book	£1.95	☐
Rebel in Time	£1.95	☐

'To The Stars' Trilogy

Homeworld	£1.95	☐
Wheelworld	£1.95	☐
Starworld	£2.50	☐

Doris Lessing
'Canopus in Argos: Archives'

Shikasta	£2.95	☐
The Marriage Between Zones Three, Four, and Five	£2.50	☐
The Sirian Experiments	£1.95	☐
The Making of the Representative for Planet 8	£2.50	☐
Documents Relating to the Sentimental Agents in the Volyen Empire	£2.50	☐

David Mace

Demon 4	£1.95	☐
Nightrider	£1.95	☐
Firelance	£2.50	☐

To order direct from the publisher just tick the titles you want and fill in the order form.

SF1282

All these books are available at your local bookshop or newsagent, or can be ordered direct from the publisher.

To order direct from the publishers just tick the titles you want and fill in the form below.

Name _____

Address _____

_____

Send to:
Grafton Cash Sales
PO Box 11, Falmouth, Cornwall TR10 9EN.

Please enclose remittance to the value of the cover price plus:

UK 55p for the first book, 22p for the second book plus 14p per copy for each additional book ordered to a maximum charge of £1.75.

BFPO and Eire 55p for the first book, 22p for the second book plus 14p per copy for the next 7 books, thereafter 8p per book.

Overseas £1.25 for the first book and 31p for each additional book.

Grafton Books reserve the right to show new retail prices on covers, which may differ from those previously advertised in the text or elsewhere.